GET IT

CW01650831

The Holistic Approach to Handwriting

The environmental, postural and physical skills required for effective and automatic handwriting

Alison Harris

and

Janet Taylor

Start Write, Stay Right
Authors: Alison Harris and Janet Taylor
All illustrations by Rebecca Barnes
Editors: Debbie Risley and Emma Caudwell

Published by:
TTS GROUP Ltd
Unit 1 Park Lane Business Park
Kirkby-in-Ashfield
Nottinghamshire NG17 9LE
www.tts-group.co.uk

British Library Cataloguing-in-Publication Data
A catalogue record for this book is available from the British Library.
ISBN: 978-1-906213-97-8

CONTENTS

FOREWARD

As Paediatric Occupational Therapists, we are regularly requested to give advice about a child who is deemed to have poor handwriting. Often, we are asked to give comment and advice from just looking at a sample of the child's writing, when the written piece of work is only the tip of the iceberg!

The Local Therapy Company was launched in March 2006. We started to offer practical training for education staff on the issues surrounding handwriting. The training courses received very positive feedback, with teachers telling us that whilst the National Literacy Strategy is high on the agenda, staff have little training on the holistic approach needed to enable a child to physically write.

This book was developed from the training course, and from the helpful input from all the delegates who attended.

We hope that you find this a useful resource in your school, and that pupils benefit from a broader approach and greater pride in their handwriting.

WHO ARE WE?

Alison Harris has worked as an Occupational Therapist since 1984. She has a background in many clinical areas, including mental health, learning disabilities and paediatrics. Her special interest is in promoting confidence and self esteem in children, with a focus on encouraging responsibility for progress and motivation coming from the child.

Janet Taylor has also worked as a Paediatric Occupational Therapist since 1988, in widely diverse settings. These include pioneering work on a Special Care Baby Unit, service development in Child Development Centres, and a broad, extensive input for children with Special Needs in both Special and Mainstream Schools.

If you would like more information on the training offered by Alison and Janet please visit www.thelocaltherapycompany.co.uk

INTRODUCTION

To understand and help a child who has handwriting difficulties, it is vitally important to observe the child writing and consider the many skills needed to write efficiently. In order to help this process, we started work on developing a checklist to help determine which key factors were problem areas for the individual child. The project grew as we linked the checklist to a resource pack of strategies, ideas and activities designed to remediate specific problem areas.

Thus, the ABC Handwriting Checklist and Framework was developed. It is not designed to teach literacy or spelling or for use with a particular handwriting scheme. It provides teachers with a holistic tool to address the practical mechanics of recording knowledge that are so often overlooked and that so deeply affect the overall skill of handwriting.

Problems are inevitably flagged up at important stages of a child's school career, such as at Year 6, or when recording is a problem at Secondary School. Worse still, it is noticed at Years 10 and 11, when approaching GCSEs.

At these stages, it is very hard to undo entrenched bad habits, and the pupil is frequently demotivated, "switched off", suffering from low self-esteem and avoiding the whole issue. This is so sad when the handwriting does not reflect the young person's true academic ability and is often as a result of ineffective holistic teaching at an early stage.

If we could share with you our best piece of advice, it would be to make "Start Write" part of your school handwriting policy and ensure pupils are using correct techniques from the beginning. Time spent on these early skills saves so much effort for both teacher and pupil having to revisit skills at a later date, when problems have arisen and disinterest has set in. Handwriting is so closely linked to self-esteem, and pupils should be encouraged to take pride in this crucial life skill. Schools should prioritise this at a high level and provide funding for varied and novel equipment to make the whole subject both interesting and rewarding. The dividends will be seen.

SETTING THE SCENE

Handwriting is undoubtedly an important skill. It is a life skill, and one that is hard to avoid. Even in this technological world, there will always be the need to make a quick note, or to complete a form, and of course, the moment when the computer fails, and important information needs recording.

Writing is a necessary skill for education, work and social life, yet in 1990, the international year of literacy, it was estimated that 4 million adults in the UK had difficulty with reading and writing.

It is a complex and difficult skill which takes several years to acquire and it is important that the skill is learned to a highly functional level, where writing is automatic, efficient and fluent. "Students who can write quickly can achieve a grade higher at GCSE regardless of academic ability." This was reported in the Times, reflecting comments made in Charter 2000. However, even pure common sense can see that efficient writing is going to improve test results, simply from the fact that the student can record a greater quantity, that they do not reduce or simplify sentences because of time restraint. If the student can write with automaticity, all their "brain energy" can be used in answering the question, and not be used up with the complex components of handwriting itself.

What makes handwriting so complex? Writing requires good postural control and shoulder stability to secure and control the use of upper limbs. It requires good wrist and hand function, with finger dexterity. It requires a functional grip on the pencil, which allows free, flowing movement and relaxed muscles. There is the no small matter of the level of cognitive skill required. The child needs to have adequate visual and perceptual skills, memory and sequencing. They need to plan ahead, whilst monitoring the present movements of the pen. There is also a requirement for good eye-hand coordination, for sensory and kinaesthetic memory. Finally, and most importantly, handwriting requires the overall integration of all these components. Without any one single skill, handwriting is challenged, and a more difficult task. It is therefore quite amazing to consider that we start teaching as early as four years of age!

"I struggled through the alphabet as if it had been a bramble-bush, getting considerably worried and scratched by every letter"

- Charles Dickens [Great Expectations]

"Learning to write is perceived to be one of the major occupations of early childhood. This intricate and complex process is one of the child's first tasks in an academic setting." [Cunningham 1992].

This is in stark contrast to some European countries such as Sweden and Denmark, where children start formal education at seven years old. These education systems are acknowledging the importance of getting the child's overall level of skill to a state of readiness through play and exploration. Virtually the entire population of Sweden is literate. [Survey July 2003]. In this country, the Rudolf Steiner Schools do not introduce reading and writing until the age of seven, and are often criticized for this.

So if the system can't be changed, then what can be done? We feel that there are many principles and ideas to introduce in the early years which will help to alleviate problems that can arise at a later date, and make the task of learning to write easier and much more fun.

Inevitably, there will be those children for whom writing is always going to be hard work, and similar principles can be used again with older children to provide another level of support and input further on in their school career. It's not an all or nothing skill to be learned in Key Stage 1 and not returned to. We need to provide greater opportunities to continue working with these children, and further support the skill of handwriting on which hangs the vast majority of their academic success.

Education staff are telling us, through our training courses, that they invariably have received little or no formal instruction on how to teach the physical aspects of handwriting. Often, experienced teaching assistants who may have Nursery Nurse Qualifications, have actually had more training than the teaching staff. This is most likely due to the fact that they have focused purely on Early Years, where correct seating and pre-writing skills are emphasized.

As we visit schools, we see many (if not even the majority of) pupils writing with poor fluency, poor physical organization, and struggling with cursive writing because of massively incorrect letter formation. The following chapters attempt to address these issues in an interesting and inclusive way.

Causes of handwriting difficulty

These fall broadly into two categories and whilst some are unavoidable, many causes can be overcome by taking on board the requests and suggestions from the "Start Write, Stay Right!" principles.

WITHIN THE EDUCATION SYSTEM

- Group teaching may miss individual need
- Child may be immature for school year
- Programme taught at inappropriate speed for the pupil
- Lack of consistency between schools affect the children who move?
- Difficulties repeating lessons missed through illness etc
- Curriculum scheme or age led opposed to child centred learning

WITHIN THE CHILD

- Poor motor control
- Poor co-ordination
- Poor stability
- Poor sensory feedback
- Slower cognitive development
- Language and communication issues
- Specific diagnoses and disability
- Behavioural issues
- Self-esteem

HOW TO USE THE BOOK!

Start Write, Stay Right! is divided into three main sections. It does exactly what the title says and provides you with lots of great resources! Start Write is about how to introduce good habits in the early stages of handwriting. Stay Right! is about how to keep the motivation going whilst encouraging any difficult areas to be resolved. The final section contains a useful selection of photocopiable worksheets.

START WRITE PAGES 11 - 35

Work through this section, assessing which parts will be useful for your class or your school. Use the "Ready to Write" assessment (page 15) to test whether your Reception class are at a point where handwriting is developmentally appropriate to be introduced. If working specifically with a small number of children, the information on topics such as core and shoulder stability on pages 27 - 29 will be useful. This section can also be used as a reference for ideas, warm ups, and activities for the youngest pupils in Primary School.

STAY RIGHT! PAGES 37 - 73

This section provides you with the very useful ABC Handwriting Checklist. A class teacher or a teaching assistant may use this with individual pupils to assess where that pupil's difficulties lie. The ABC Handwriting Checklist (page 40 - 43) enables the teacher to see the precise area of need. In many cases, this can be almost instantly solved when it has at last been defined! Whatever the outcome of the assessment, you will find answers in the following section which is the Handwriting Framework on pages 44 - 52. This invaluable piece of information signposts the teacher to clear instruction on how to manage and deal with the child's area of difficulty.

WORKSHEETS PAGES 75 - 95

And finally lots of photocopiable worksheets for immediate use! These great worksheets will enable you to develop and expand the Start Write, Stay Right principles.

As Paediatric Occupational Therapists, we are asked for help and advice when handwriting problems occur. However, a high percentage of these difficulties could have been prevented if the child had started out on the complex process of learning to handwrite with some basic fundamentals established. This may initially delay the start of formal handwriting tuition, but we strongly advise that the child gets the best start, and subsequently potential difficulties may not transpire.

Readiness for writing

Children develop at different rates and at school entry, each child already has differing abilities. Levels of maturity also vary widely. An August birthday puts some children at an immediate disadvantage. It is important to assess each child as to their readiness to learn to write. Small groups can then set-off on this complex task at a time that is right for them, rather than a whole class because "that always happens the second week after half term!"

The "Ready to Write" checklist (see page 15) sums up the most important factors in determining if the child is ready to write. Time needs to be given to developing these early skills in a fun and attractive way. This can easily be done in an Early Years environment, it is much harder to backtrack in later years when problems are highlighted.

1. IS A CHILD READY TO WRITE?

Each child must be assessed as an individual, not as a class group, or whole year group. The Ready to Write Checklist highlights seven key areas to determine a child's readiness to write.

1. Is the child able to sit correctly and comfortably on a chair and use both hands freely?

Many a time, we have visited schools and seen children sitting on a folded leg, half on/half off a chair, with the chair on two legs, or lying across a table. Children inevitably fidget and change positions, at an early age, it is important that a child appreciates the need for good sitting when working. On many occasions when working with a child, they have suddenly slipped off their chair. It seems improbable, but it regularly happens!

2. Is the child able to use each hand independently?

Many Early Years and pre-school activities encourage this. We suggest giving children every opportunity for sand and water play with containers, buckets and spades, play dough with cutters and rolling pins, construction toys, stencils and shapes to draw around. All these activities promote the use of each hand doing a different task. Activities such as threading beads, assembling nuts and bolts and winding string on a bobbin will easily confirm if a child has developed this skill.

"We don't know why her writing is so untidy..."

3. Has the child developed a neat, functional pencil grip?

A well developed pencil grip is vitally important for a correct tripod pencil grip. Many children are unable to hold their pencil correctly when starting to learn to write and therefore acquire an incorrect grip. Whilst initially this may be acceptable, a poor or incorrect grip will soon become habitual and will interfere with the flow, speed, fluency and efficiency of cursive writing. Activities to practice and assess pincer grip include:

Moving dried peas from dish to dish	Picking up small beads
Popping bubble wrap	Posting coins
Turning over counters	Rolling dough into small balls

4. Has the child developed hand dominance?

Dominance is important in that each hand becomes skilful in a particular role, movement, deed or action. It allows complex tasks to be completed quickly, easily and in a refined style. Changing hand dominance disturbs the acquisition of skill. Having said that, many people do certain individual tasks with their non-dominant hand. This is not a problem if that task is always done in that way. If a child has not developed hand dominance, it is advisable to let the child practice activities using their hands together in the same way.

Examples:

Rolling dough using a rolling pin

Pouring water/sand from containers in each hand at the same time

Symmetrical clapping games

Moving bricks from each side to the middle, both hands moving at the same time

Doodling the same free pattern with both hands mirroring each other

Rolling a large ball with two hands

It soon became obvious which was Oliver's dominant hand.

Over time, the task should become quicker and easier with one hand taking the lead, and thereby becoming the dominant hand.

5. Has the child awareness of "up" and "down"?

In order to follow directions and be able to appreciate how shapes are formed, the child needs to have basic perceptual skills. These develop through use of jigsaws, construction toys, simple board games, colouring and general play such as dolls house, toy garage, action songs and using the slide and climbing frame. If a child has regular access to a wide range of differing activities, spatial perceptual skills will normally develop alongside.

6. Can the child copy basic strokes and symbols?

Emergent writing and drawing is often part of the process of being ready to formally start to learn to write. If a child is not keen on any pencil skills, it's a clear indication that more time is needed for play, and stimulating activities which will encourage their interest.

For a child to start the process of letter formation, he or she must be able to make a range of different marks using a pencil on paper. The child therefore has the ability to appreciate basic form and shape, and move the pencil as desired. Beery (1989) and Maeland (1992) found that the ability to copy (not imitate) eight basic forms was significant in predicting the child's ability to learn to write.

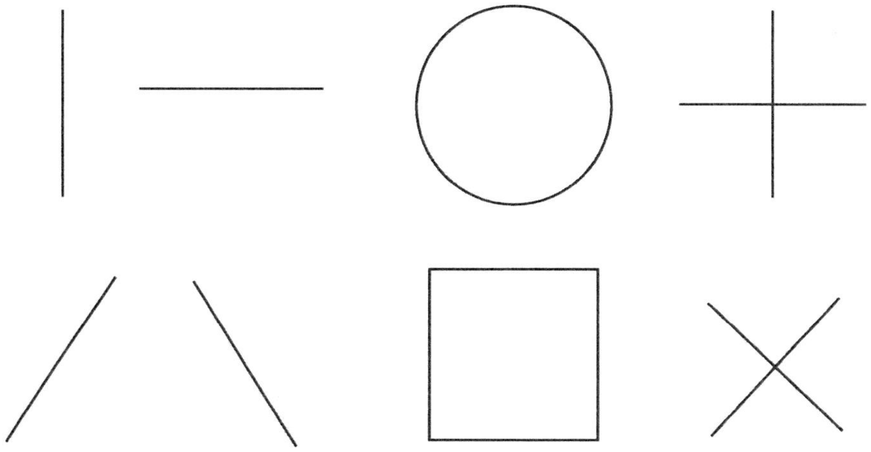

7.Can the child follow instructions?

This is very much linked with a child's desire and motivation to write. Children who have difficulty sitting still, listening, and who do not have the required fine motor skills will quickly switch off and see handwriting as something to be avoided! A child needs to be interested in mark making and learning to write and be able to follow the basic tasks of good sitting, correct pencil grip and placement of paper. They also need to be able to follow the directions given for letter formation.

A motivated child who is responsive to directions and guidance will be able to learn and gain success more easily.

Ready to Write Assessment

Based on the seven points discussed, this is a quick and simple checklist which can be administered by a class teacher or by a teaching assistant. It highlights if the child is developmentally ready to learn handwriting. Have they got the physical skills, stability and strength that will be required? As therapists, our strongly held opinion and recommendations are that if a child is not ready to write, more work and time needs to be devoted to play. Rushing into handwriting can lead to frustration, lack of interest and even loss of motivation resulting in the development of poor behaviour and avoidance strategies.

Ready to Write Checklist

Name: Date of Birth:

NB. Has vision been checked?	Y	N
Are glasses worn if required?	Y	N
1. Ability to sit on a chair and use both arms freely?	Y	N
2 Ability to use each hand independently doing a different task e.g. sharpen a pencil, thread beads, assemble nuts and bolts?	Y	N
3. Can the child grasp and release small objects easily and fluently using a neat pincer grip?	Y	N
4. Hand dominance identified or emerging?	Y	N
5. Awareness of direction i.e. up and down, top and bottom?	Y	N
6. Ability and wish to follow instructions?	Y	N
7. Can the child copy basic strokes and symbols?	Y	N

(Ref: Beery 1989; Maeland 1992) Pls tick as appropriate:

2. THE FUNDAMENTALS OF EARLY HANDWRITING

There are many fundamental factors which influence the success of handwriting. These can be integrated and used within any scheme of plan. They often appear very obvious, but our workload and experience tells us that many of these issues are either overlooked or not given a high enough degree of importance.

Pencil grip

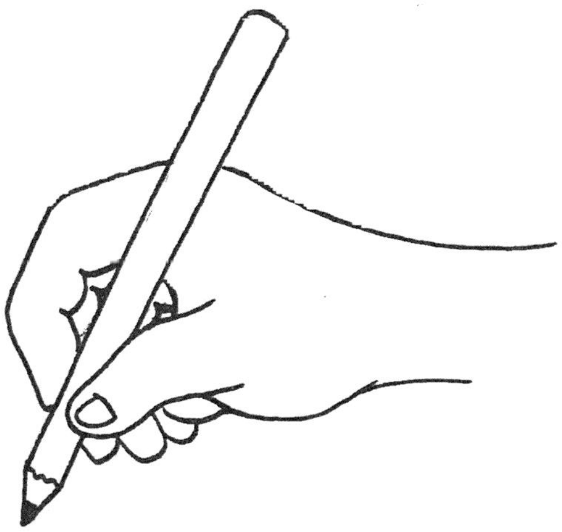

How many children are not actively, and persistently taught how to hold their pencil correctly? The answer must be many, judging by the huge numbers of incorrect grips that we see.

It is important to teach the child how to hold their pencil and why it is so important.

One easy way to teach this skill is:

A) Lay the pencil down pointing to the child's tummy

B) "Pinch the pencil near the writing point" (mark with tape or a band)

C) Pick it up to swing over and to sit comfortably in the web space

D) Sit it on the middle finger

You may feel that this may not be a big issue at this point in time, but starting off with good habits is far easier than trying to resolve them later. Many children could manage with an incorrect grip for a long period of time, even into Year 2, but they will meet a growing requirement for speed, control, fluency and cursive movement which they will struggle to perform without a good tripod pencil grip.

A tripod grip is vital for quick, efficient, fluent pencil movement. The thumb leads circular movements primarily. The index finger makes firm push/pull movements. The middle finger supports the writing tool, whilst allowing these ranges of movements.

Provide a wide range of pencils and crayons, with and without plastic grips, so that each child can choose which they feel comfortable with. It is very important to persist in correcting and working towards a tripod grip at an early stage. Use a correct grip to colour, do-dot-to-dots, mazes, tracking, stencils and pre-writing patterns. Any fun pencil activity can be used to establish the tripod grip prior to introducing the further complications of letter formation.

Colouring

Some children enjoy colouring and some don't! However, it is an excellent way to develop eye-hand co-ordination and pencil control. White paper and broken wax crayons soon lose their appeal. Try to vary the colour and type of paper and use attractive crayons, chalks, paints and so on. Thick outlines with a marker pen (1cm thick) can produce a better result for a child with poor control. Large A4 pictures with big shapes to colour can be boring, so try smaller pictures, A5 size, with smaller parts which can be completed in less time and give a better result.

Directional colouring encourages the good finger movements required for pencil control. Use any shape, and mark with lines in one direction. Help the child to anchor their hand by the shape, and to colour in the shape only in the direction of the lines. Vary the direction to include vertical, horizontal and diagonal movements.

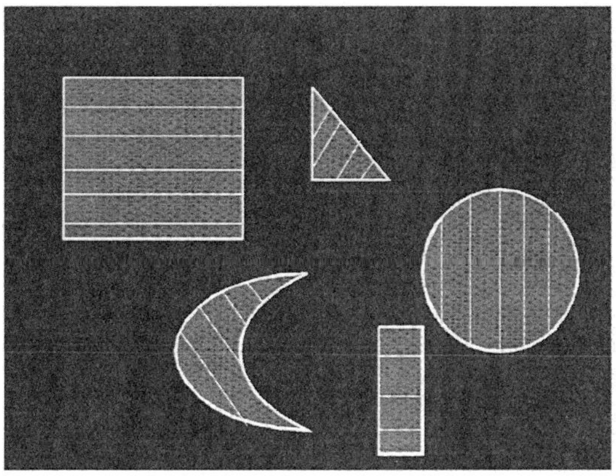

Curly drawings using continuous loops encourage small circular movements and can be done in clockwise or anti-clockwise directions. This is a great warm up exercise for small fingers.

Keep on colouring and drawing, using fun activities until the child automatically uses a dynamic tripod grip. Ensure the fingers and hand are doing the work (not the arm and shoulder).

ACTIVITIES TO IMPROVE COLOURING

Use new, attractive crayons and colouring pens in an attractive container. i.e. make it special!

Consider which crayons will be best for the child's developmental level

-chunky wax crayons

-thin wax crayons

-fat or thin pencil crayons

-flow of colour - some crayons need increased pressure to get a good result of colour

Use pictures appropriate for the child, both in style, detail and size.

Stationers and supermarkets sell simple picture colouring books on good quality paper.

Use clear PVA glue to outline a simple shape or picture. This provides a ridge to colour up to and give tactile feedback if coloured over.

Show the child how to colour the edges before moving into the middle area.

Use very thick (1cm) wide outlines if necessary. This gives a wide margin for error and the child sees better results.

Practice colouring along curved lines.

Practice colouring in one direction whilst moving the fingers and hand in order to colour in a larger area.

Practice colouring in shapes with strokes going in one direction, but change direction for a different shape eg. Horizontal, vertical and diagonal.

Practice colouring in neatly but quickly. Use a timer to promote speed, especially for the child who spends a long time colouring a small area.

To increase crayon pressure try tactile rubbings or working towards making a stronger colour on the page.

Practice colouring from a strong colour (heavy pressure) to a light shade (light pressure).

Pre-writing patterns

There are many books and worksheets available with mazes, tracking patterns and pre-writing patterns. Pre-writing patterns develop the child's ability to discriminate size, shape and form. It also develops pencil movement, control, planning and directionality. When practising pre-writing patterns, it is important to keep the emphasis on size and shape. Speed then naturally follows on.

Tables and Chairs

Tables and chairs must be at the correct height for the child, whatever their age or year group. Children vary enormously in height even at school entry. For particularly tall or small children, try swapping a table and chairs with the next year group, up or down, so that all children can be accommodated.

The ideal sitting position is:

- The back being supported by a chair of correct depth.
- Hips, knees and ankles at 90°
- Table height should be 6cm higher than the elbow

If the table is too high or low, sitting posture and shoulder position is affected and this in turn affects hand function.

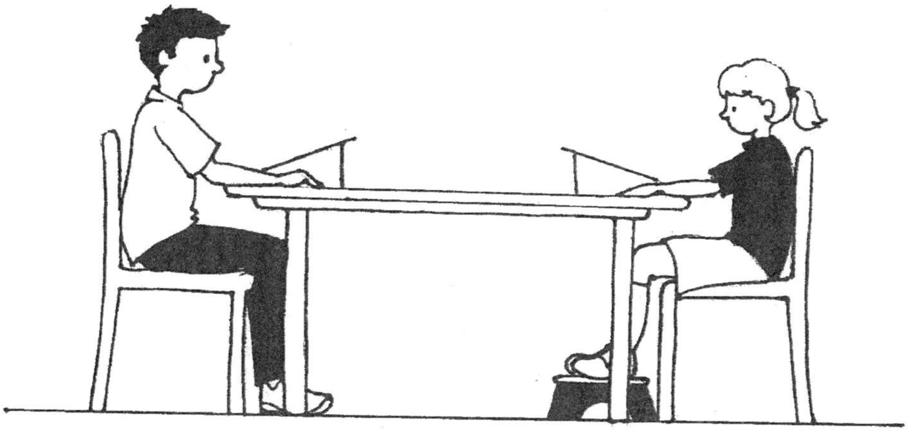

Make sure children have enough space when working at the table. When class numbers have been particularly high, we have seen children sharing space or sitting at the corner of a table. Also consider left handers, who need to be on the end of a table, or sat next to another left hander, rather than fighting for elbow room with a right handed child.

3. STRUCTURED SMALL STAGES

1. Consider your own writing - it MUST reflect what you are teaching

When children are ready for handwriting, and starting off on your writing scheme, it is important that letter formation is addressed consistently. Ensure that your writing, and the writing of other classroom staff, on wall displays and marking is consistent and reflects what is being taught.

2. Consider a parent's evening for handwriting

Most parents are keen to help their children but may unwittingly teach the child incorrect letter formation.

Inform parents about appropriate and beneficial play activities for this stage, and share individual targets for each child.

3. Movement

Movement needs to be correct and is more important than neatness at this stage. Correct letter formation is of prime importance as incorrect letter formation prevents cursive writing and the more habitual it becomes, the harder it is to correct.

Practice is the only way to acquire a physical skill - but you must practise correctly and consistently

4. Keep it LARGE

Keep the movements large so it comes from the shoulder and the whole arm feels the shape.

5. Multi-sensory activities

Multi-sensory activities help to lay down the "movement memory" - see page 24 for multi-sensory ideas.

6. Handwriting lessons must be short

Keeping the handwriting lesson short, 10 minutes daily, helps keep the children interested. Little and often prevents loss of interest and reinforces all the Start Write principles on a regular basis.

4. MULTI-SENSORY!

Don't stick to tables!

In the Early Years environment, writing practice does not have to be at the table. Children can work standing up at the board, easel, or wall. Even a water pistol can be used in the play ground for patterns and letter formation. Some children benefit from lying on their tummies, propped up on elbows to draw, colour and write. This encourages shoulder stability and the arm triangle which is the space between the arm and the body. This allows fluent writing movement across the paper.

Paper and pencil is boring! Use interesting crayons, bright colours, marker pens, glitter glue, highlighters, paints and chalks.

Chalk on sugar paper gives particularly good sensory feedback.

Try writing with:

- fingers in sand or gunge trays,
- a stick in rolled out dough,
- torch on a dark wall or curtain,
- ribbon stick or streamer,
- light sticks such as Star Wars and similar.

5. WARM UPS FOR LITTLE HANDS!

Small hands often don't have the strength and stamina to write for long periods. A few warm up exercises help to wake up hand muscles ready for writing and relax them at the end of the session.

- Thumbs up

- Fist and Stretch

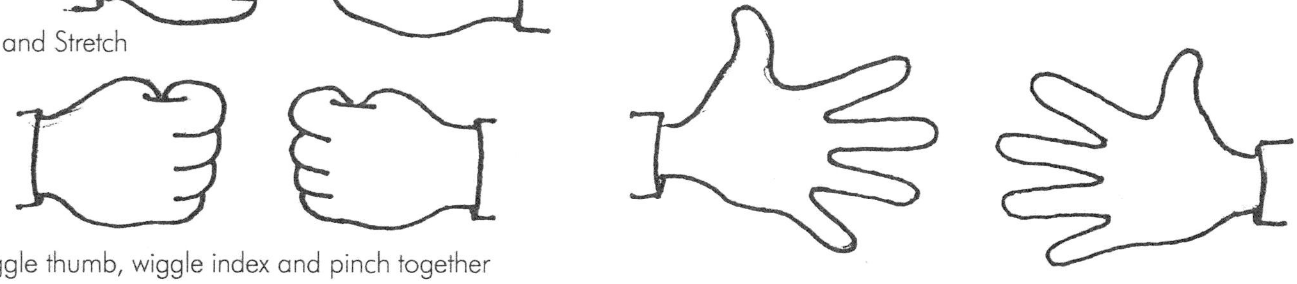

- Wiggle thumb, wiggle index and pinch together
- Ducks beaks
- Touch each finger to thumb

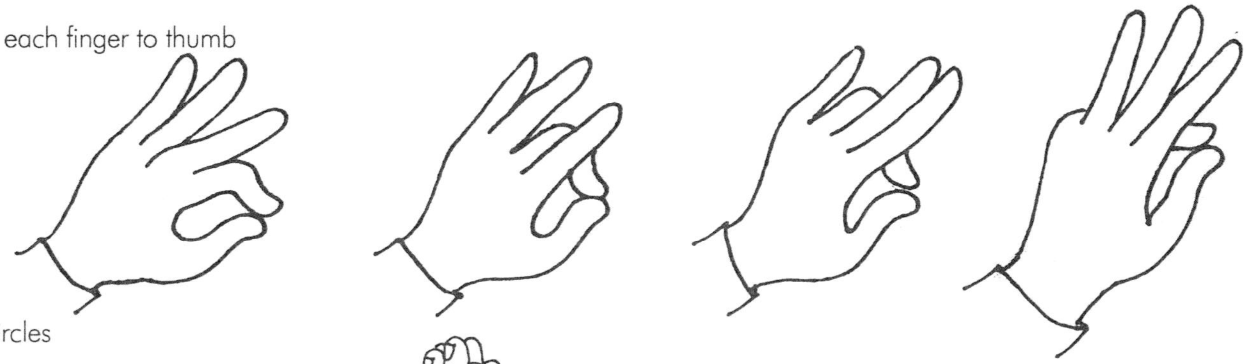

- Arm circles
- Push hands together then shake out

- Finger stretch under thighs
  palms face down touching the chair

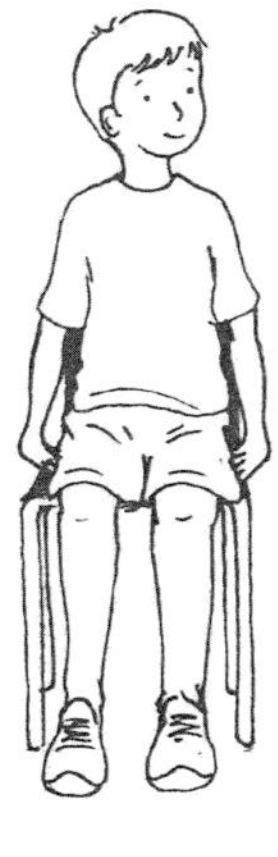

- Pick up pen, arrange fingers ready to start!

Writing Rap

Here's a super example of a warm up rap given to us by a colleague. We thought it was wonderful and have included it, with kind permission, so other children could learn the rap and enjoy it too!

Adapted from Ann Markee, Paediatric Physiotherapist, Rugby Handwriting Interest Group by Andrea Bennington, Advisory Teacher for Children with Physical Disabilities

A rap to help children sit correctly when writing

1, 2, 3, 4

Are your feet flat on the floor?

5, 6, 7, 8

Is your back nice and straight?

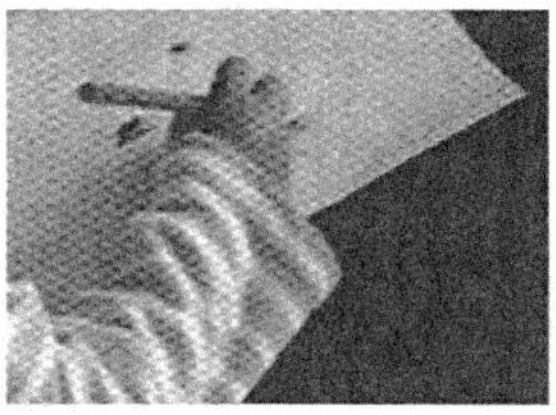

9, 10, 11, 12

Check the way your pencil's held

13, 14, 15, 16

Is your paper correctly seen?

17, 18, 19, 20

Now you're ready to write aplenty

6. DEVELOPING CORE AND SHOULDER STABILITY

Core stability

Core stability is the ability to control the position and movement of the body's centre. It provides the foundation for all arm and leg movements. In conjunction with shoulder stability, core stability provides the firm base for control in handwriting and fine motor skills.

Exercises to develop core stability can also provide proprioceptive feedback (the knowledge of the body's position through joint and muscle movement). The development of core stability is fundamental in physical development and should be taken as a primary and important factor in considering a child's functional skills. Poor core stability in itself leads to poor shoulder stability as the shoulders do not have a firm base.

Exercises to help

Checking that a child can perform these exercises well is a helpful initial assessment. To improve core stability, exercises need to be done regularly, preferably daily (and at a minimum of three times a week). Benefits can be seen quite quickly and there are long term gains in developing a firm core.

All exercises should be done slowly in a controlled manner. Aim for quality not quantity.

Pushing against a partner

Kneel up tall (thighs, hips and trunk in straight line). With both palms against partners palms, push in a long sustained push. Do not lock elbows. Do not pulse push, but keep one long push going for a count of 10. Relax and repeat three times.

Kneel to stand

Start in a high kneel position and then move slowly to a standing position. Slowly go back down to half kneel and then back to starting position. Do not lean on your knees or touch the floor. If necessary fold arms, or for a harder exercise, hold arms raised above head.

Statues

Stand in a pose like a soldier holding a sword and a shield. Keep totally still as your partner tries to move you by gentle pushing/bending on arms, legs or trunk. You are made of stone, you mustn't move!

Four point kneeling

Kneel with hands on the floor directly under shoulders, and knees directly under thighs. Push the floor away. Hold for a count of 5. Relax and repeat 5 times.

Banana bend

Lie on the floor on your stomach, with arms stretched out straight above head. Keeps arms and legs straight and raise them all off the floor for a count of 10. Relax.
Repeat 3 times.

SHOULDER STABILITY

Shoulder stability is vital for good hand control. It makes sense that if the base of the arm is not strong, there can be little or no accuracy in hand skills. If a child clamps their arm into their trunk to have control, this may indicate a potential problem with shoulder stability.

Standing to write or draw at a vertical surface develops strength around the shoulder.

Playing games on all fours is also helpful. Try playing Jenga or setting up dominoes whilst on all fours. These can also be good activities to suggest for home.

Exercises to help

Arm circles

Hold arms out straight at the side. Movement is to come from the shoulder and arms should remain straight throughout. Start by making circles which are tennis ball sized. Go forwards and backwards. Then make the circle bigger maybe car tyre size, and then onto tractor wheel size. Aim for 1 min +.

Push-ups against the wall

Stand a stride distance away from the wall, facing the wall with both arms holding body away from the wall. SLOWLY bend elbows and reach towards wall. Keep the movement controlled and slow. Touch the tip of your nose to the wall, and then push SLOWLY back to arms in full stretch position. Repeat 10 times.

Pushing against a partner

Kneel up tall (thighs, hips and trunk in straight line). With both palms against partners palms, push in a long sustained push. Do not lock elbows. Do not pulse push, but keep one long push going for a count of 10. Relax and repeat three times.

HANDWRITING WORKOUT!

A quick workout before starting to write which is suitable for a group sitting at a table ready to start the session.

- Shrug shoulders up to ears and down (10 times)
- Put hands together at chest level and push together for a count of 5
- Circle wrists in both directions for a count of 10
- Make a fist tightly and then spread fingers wide (5 times)
- Put thumbs up and wriggle round in a circle and up and down
- Make a duck beak.....
- Use your duck beaks to "quack" your fingers to yourself
- Use your duck beaks to "quack" to your teacher
- Move each finger to touch your thumb one at a time
- Make owl eyes with thumb and first finger
- Shake out your hands up in the air

7. LETTER FAMILIES

Your school's writing scheme may well dictate the order in which to teach letters or the groups that they are presented in. This can include letters by height, by direction of movement, and length below the line. Children will start to learn at very different rates, some remembering letters quickly, and others needing lots of repetition. Multi-sensory work is good for the individual letters that cause a particular problem.

Letter formation needs to be corrected at this stage, just as you would correct spellings.

It can be beneficial to move on to learning or writing two letters together as soon as possible as on, learning one letter in isolation can be rather pointless. Commonly paired letters can be useful to reinforce reading and spelling.

st th tr sh ch

an in of to

It can also be helpful to use similarly formed letters, or contrasting letters, which reinforce the difference in shape and formation.

mn ad go do fs

gh sp re mo qu

Verbalisation

Practising letter formations with a verbalisation, i.e. saying sounds out loud to assist, can be beneficial except when every letter sounds the same! What does " around, up, down and flick!" really mean? This sounds about right for the description of many letter movements. Consider just saying the letter sound as the letter is formed. Be aware of the instructions you are giving, and listen to them with a child's ear. Be sure they make sense and are helpful. Keep it simple, but be creative.

For example, for an "a" 'all around the apple and down the leaf'.

Schemes such as "Letterland" and "Jolly Phonics" make letter shapes link to sounds and actions and they have invaluable components to assist in your particular scheme. With characterisations, the letters become meaningful and memorable.

'all around the apple and down the leaf'

8. WRITING TOOLS

Use a variety of pencils, crayons and other mark making tools. Have a selection of grips and encourage the child to choose a tool that suits them. Fatter barrelled pencils are available in Early Years, but it would be great to have them throughout KS1, if not KS2 as well. Why is there a rush to put thin pencils into small hands? As adults, we often choose a shaped pen, or one with a soft grip so why shouldn't each child have this choice?

At Junior age, children are often allowed to bring in their own pencils and pens, which unfortunately are not always the best choices in terms of ergonomics. They often have top heavy ornaments, dangling beads, and under or over sized lengths.

Encourage children to be particular about what they use to write with and to be aware what a negative effect a pen can have on presentation. We need to teach pride in presentation from an early age. This means providing good pencils, pens and crayons in school in contrast to the common provision of the cheapest.

Daisy couldn't wait to try her new pencil in handwriting practice!

Paper and exercise books

The choice of lined or unlined paper is often a matter of School Policy and is frequently class or subject led. Some pupils will need the lines to keep their writing straight and help them to be uniform in letter size. Others will find lines a constriction which is inappropriate to their stage of writing skill. Different children need different tools. Try whenever possible to consider the options, and allow the child to have the correct paper or book type for their ability or style.

What is to be gained from either using lined or unlined paper?

What does the individual child need?

If the school policy is not bringing out the pupil's best handwriting,
can you discuss this as a staff group?

9. HOW TO MOTIVATE THE UNMOTIVATED

The young child who prefers to play!

Children can have a lack of interest in pen and paper activities, and early writing tasks for a number of reasons. If you can gain an idea of why the child is reluctant to participate or is disinterested, it will obviously help when trying to address this. Reasons may include:

- Activity appears boring and uninteresting
- Lots more exciting things to do especially in the nursery setting
- Lack of relevance
- Task has been too difficult in the past
- Pressure from family members to do the task for intense periods

Suggestions

1. Make the task attractive and interesting. Many nursery and reception settings still have rough pieces of scrap paper, dried up felt tip pens, broken crayons and old wax crayons on the drawing table. Invest in a range of brightly coloured paper, glitter pens and paints, tubes of fluorescent paint, finger-paints etc.
2. Don't stick to tables, use large pieces of paper to cover a wall and let the children decorate the wall.
3. Use chalkboards, white boards, and the playground floor or school wall. If the child enjoys computers use a simple drawing or art programme. Try drawing shapes, letters and numbers in a sand tray or in a paint tray.
4. Develop the activity into a topic which will interest that child i.e. on a piece of superman wall paper circling the stars, or drawing connecting lines from object to object. Draw a picture of a lion, then draw a square cage and put in the vertical bars. Give the fairy lots of curly hair.
5. Build the drawing or writing activity into a bigger activity e.g. use the dressing up clothes to become a builder and draw the house to be built or add onto a basic shape roof, windows, chimney, door, path etc.

6. Explain to the child what they are to do and that it is just that. Give the activity a definite start and finish so they will be likely to co-operate knowing they only need to complete small stages.
7. Make up activities or tasks that will be meaningful to the child. Use topics and subjects that interest them. When collecting a snack or a drink they have to put a cross or mark on a chart or next to their name. When going to use the racing car in the playground they have to sign it out and in with whatever is appropriate.
8. Make a personal workbook. Put in pictures of the child, family, pets, toys and places. Use this to develop the writing activity, whether it be labelling, practising numbers or linking pictures with prewriting patterns.
9. A good strategy for children who tend to stick to their favourite activity is to plan with them a timetable e.g. sand and water, lego and bikes until snack time, and then a short painting task, outdoor toys and book corner.
10. Keep the activity at the level for that child. It is important that they have continued and consistent success. Identify very small achievable stages and plan activities to meet these.
11. Give appropriate rewards. Five minutes doing the identified drawing or writing task and then for example, time on the computer.
12. Work on a 1:1 with the child when drawing and writing. Draw with them an object of their choice and get them to contribute, adding parts and shapes etc. This is good for children who find drawing difficult. Teach them basic forms so they can draw some of the basic ideas e.g. person, vehicle, animal, building.
13. Encourage drawing by using collage as starting points e.g. stick on two circles for head and body and the child adds features, or a square and a triangle for a roof.
14. Give parents and carers advice and support. Make suggestions on what they can do and give them ideas of alternative activities to take the focus off pen and paper writing activities.

STAY RIGHT!

Even when all the principles of 'Start Write' have been applied, some pupils will have experienced considerable difficulty learning the complex skill of handwriting. It is important to have a different programme suited to the older child. It needs to consider the young person's self esteem and provide an encouraging approach.

Research (and common sense) indicates that a pupil with smooth, fluent and automatic handwriting is going to do better in test situations, purely because they can apply their brain energy to the subject being tested. This information must surely influence schools to try again with pupils higher up the education system. Time should be invested to assess and help improve their handwriting skills.

Pupils will have a varying level of skill for many reasons. Some may have missed large chunks of their education through illness, whilst others may have moved from school to school and attempted to keep up with the demands of various handwriting styles. For whatever reason, pupils deserve another chance to develop this crucial skill.

Helping the older child with their handwriting

By late Key Stage 2, handwriting styles are likely to be entrenched, and errors have become habitual. The motivation of the pupil is paramount. Self assessment should be encouraged, and the decision to work on this skill is best if it comes from the pupil themselves. Gentle encouragement and clear methods of support from the teacher are also very important. Perhaps one way of motivating the young person is to suggest that there is a need for refinement, rather than "starting again!" For example, emphasis can be placed on speed, which most pupils will realise is going to directly benefit them with their note taking in class. Legibility is also of great importance. Marks may be lost if an examiner is unable to decipher the writing.

It is vital to help an older pupil see the logic and reasoning for going back to basics with handwriting. It can be highly beneficial to spend time discussing and agreeing plans in order to motivate the young person, and also to indicate the level of support that you are willing to provide.

Advice

- Use the Handwriting ABC checklist (see page 40 - 43) to assess where the problem lies. It may be that resolution can be found by improving physical skills such as core stability, or through the use of better equipment.
- At this stage it is pointless to try to change pencil grip. Assessment of posture, shoulder and core stability and the equipment used is likely to be more helpful.
- If the pupil's handwriting is fluent, legible and of reasonable speed, a few badly formed letters are not going to drastically affect speed and should be ignored.
- In some cases, there may be major issues with written recording, to the extent that the pupil's cognitive understanding and ability is not reflected in written work. It may be helpful to consider the use of a Dictaphone, particularly for recording instructions and home work. Ideas may also be recorded, reducing the amount of writing that is expected to be produced.

- Consider a bullet point technique for recording lesson content. A more able student may well be able to summarise content into short, sharp points.
- Mind mapping has been developed as a useful technique for demonstrating ideas, and links in thought processes, and requires considerably less handwritten recording than handwriting in long hand.
- It is VITAL that the pupil is taught these techniques and supported whilst they begin using them. A supportive teacher can provide guidance and improve technique quickly.
- It is also very important that all members of teaching staff are aware of the techniques that will be used. There should be clarity about the acceptable forms of recording, and this should be organized and put in place by a keyworker for the pupil. This is particularly crucial at Secondary level.
- Another popular solution for ensuring that the pupil has a good set of notes to learn and revise from, is for the teacher to provide a copy of lesson content as a matter of routine. This should be available to all pupils, and not just those who are having difficulty with their handwriting.
- If the difficulties seem unlikely to change, and are affecting confidence and motivation to a great extent, it is advisable to move on to using IT as soon as possible. This may include predictive software and in extreme cases, may require voice recognition software.

The important rule of thumb is:

Does the pupil's recording reflect their level of knowledge? If not, do something about it!

1. HANDWRITING ABC CHECKLIST AND FRAMEWORK

The ABC Handwriting Checklist and Framework is a holistic, practical tool designed to identify difficulties of handwriting and give suggestions and advice on how to approach the issue.

The Checklist can be used by teachers or teaching assistants to identify problem areas that an individual child may have. It can be completed over one session, but it is recommended that the checklist is carried out by observing the child writing over two or three lessons, particularly if the child moves classrooms and has different teachers for other subjects.

The Checklist is divided into three areas - Environment, Posture and Writing Product. It is important to be aware that a child's difficulties could fall into mainly one area or be scattered over all three sections. By accurately identifying the difficult areas, clear targets can be set and worked towards in small achievable stages. After a period of intervention, the ABC Checklist can be repeated to review if targets have been achieved and difficulties resolved.

The Handwriting ABC Framework (see pages 44 - 52) is linked to the checklist by reference number and letter. This means that for all the observations highlighted as difficulties, there are linked suggestions on the Framework to help remediate and address the issues. Recommendations and advice are by no means complete and conclusive. Experienced teachers and TAs will no doubt have their own tried and tested means of helping with problem areas. Many of the activities, ideas and resources have been gathered from years of classroom experience, and working alongside respected members of teaching staff.

HANDWRITING ABC CHECKLIST

Name: ______________________ Date: ______________________

School/Class: ______________________ DOB/Age ______________________

A	ENVIRONMENTAL	COMMENTS
A1	Chair Size: the chair needs to be the correct height for the child. Bottom and thighs on the chair, knees at 90°, feet flat on the floor.	
A2	Table Size: the table needs to be the correct height – at the child's elbow level, forearm flat on the table.	
A3	Writing Tool: what does he/she write with pen/pencil, type of pen/pencil, thick/thin, quality of lead. Avoid fashion item!	
A4	Paper/book: size of book, paper, quality of paper, plain, lined.	
A5	Distractions: position in class, peers, windows, displays, doors, noise.	
A6	Position in class: left hander? Table corner? Can they access drawers/trays?	

B	POSTURE/POSITIONS/ MOTOR SKILLS	COMMENTS
B1	Sitting posture: slumped? Leaning to side? Always adjusting position?	
B2	Shoulder position: raised shoulders? Relaxed? Movement?	
B3	Arm position: arm resting on table? Held to side or at 45° angle? Arm movements?	
B4	Wrist position: hand resting on its side? Wrist bent? Wrist movements?	
B5	Finger movements: fingers moving to guide the pen? Fingers straight or bent?	
B6	Pencil grip: tripod grip/3 finger grip/wrapped thumb? Pen resting in web space?	

B7	Tension of grip: loose, tight, hand ache. Tremor?	
B8	Handedness: swapping/consistent with other activities such as cutting?	
B9	Use of supporting hand Yes/No.	
B10	Position of book: does child adjust paper/book, or do they lean?	
B11	Associated movements: tongue poking/grimace/feet position/jaw moving?	
C	**THE FINISHED RESULT: WRITING PRODUCT**	**COMMENTS**
C1	Letter formation: are all letters correctly formed. List any problems noted.	
C2	Does the writing show: • Good curves • Ascenders • Descenders	
C3	Is there letter closure?	
C4	Is there any ambiguity? Could some letters be read as an alternative letter eg. v and r, o and a.	
C5	Are there any reversals? List them.	
C6	Are letters appropriately spaced?	
C7	Are words appropriately spaced?	
C8	Is there correct use of upper and lower case letters?	
C9	Is punctuation used correctly?	
C10	Is the writing consistent or does it change in style, presentation and neatness?	
C11	Pencil pressure: faint or heavy? Check under the paper to see increased pressure.	
C12	Writing style: cursive, print, mixture.	

HANDWRITING ABC CHECKLIST

C13	Size of writing: size of individual letters.	
C14	Endurance: how much does the child write before tiring?	
C15	Speed: How quickly can the child write? You may wish to measure using the speed test.	

AGE	6	7	8	9	10	13	16	
words per minute	4	6	7	9	10	15	20	

FURTHER COMMENTS:

TARGETS:

Review Date:

Signed:

Checklist	ENVIRONMENTAL
A1 A2 C10	**Table and Chairs** OBSERVE YOUR PUPILS! Any swinging feet? Hooking feet around chair legs for stability? Elbows wide apart or raised shoulders (due to table being too high)? Rounding of back? (table too low). Consider swapping a table and set of chairs with another year group so that you can provide different heights for different height pupils. Feet need to be on the floor to a) help with comfort b) enable change of position and c) provide stability and a good base. Cut out tables can be helpful with Foundation stage children. A particularly small child may need a foot box, or a chair with an inbuilt footrest (see page 21 for further details). Look for "arm triangle" where arm is held out and away from the body in a triangle. This indicates enough stability at the shoulder and is the best posture for writing. Lying on the stomach to draw encourages this 'arm triangle' and can be useful to do with younger pupils. It also encourages shoulder stability. If there is no 'arm triangle', it may indicate a lack of shoulder stability, and you may wish to work on this before proceeding. See page 29 for suggested exercises.
A3 C10	**Writing Tools** The younger child needs chunky crayons and pencils as their hands are immature, possibly quite weak in grip strength. The young child is learning new motor movements which are not yet refined, a larger tool is easier to learn with. Triangular pens and crayons promote a tripod grip and can be preferable to using plastic grips which can often just be something extra to fiddle with! Some children love grips. Try them! 2B or even 4B pencils can be helpful as an early learning tool as they make a better pencil mark when less pressure is applied. Teach pupils to use a good tool - they need to be sharp and manageable in the hand. Fashion items are not usually beneficial for writing. This applies just as importantly later on when biros should be avoided as they tend to be spidery and can be blotchy. Provide a variety of pencils and crayons throughout KS1. If it is normal to use varying tools, there is less stigma about still using a chunky pen. Explain to pupils that they need to consider what pen or pencil makes their writing best. **Pen Licences** A huge area for obliterating self-esteem as the lack of a licence can give a daily message that their writing is not good enough. Consider alternatives; - a whole class drive to make improvements ready to move onto pens - weaker writers may be able to use pens in specific handwriting lessons - weaker writers may use pens in numeracy where there is less recording - consider everyone using a pen for copying up best work - consider everyone using a pen for display work

Checklist ENVIRONMENTAL

A4

Paper/book

Lined or unlined - this is often a school policy decision. Child centred learning should look at each individual's needs and some pupils will be better with lined, and some with unlined. Can you provide lined/unlined for different topics e.g. lined for literacy and unlined for topic work?

Size of book

A4 books can be far too large for younger children and encourages them to stand to reach, thereby undoing all your good work on posture and position.

Paper position:

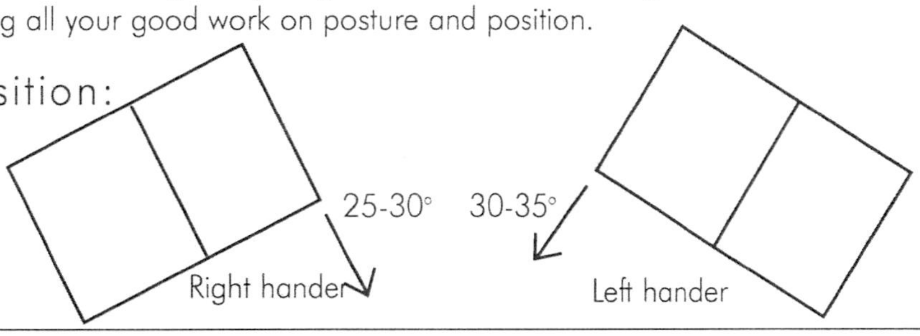

- Paper should be positioned to the right/left of the pupil's midline.
- It should enable the writing hand to be in a straight line from the elbow, through a relaxed wrist.
- The forearm should be rested on the table.
- The trunk should not need to move in any way.
- There should be no need to cross the midline if positioned properly.

This helps to

- see what you are writing
- not smudge (particularly left handers)
- reduce fatigue
- provides best efficiency with least effort

Suggestions:

- Use tape on desk to mark an area
- Use tape to indicate where to place paper/ book

Checklist	ENVIRONMENTAL
A5	**Distractions** Is the child sat in a distracting situation? Near the pencil sharpener? Or near the window where there is a mechanical digger working? Near the toilets? Next to the trays/drawers? Next to a 'hands on display'? Some children will cope with distractions a lot better than others so, give positioning careful thought.
A6	**Position in class** - Consider position on the table especially if the child is left handed. Sit them at the end of a table, not next to a right hander so they have the space they need. - Are they directly facing the board for copying or handwriting practice? Carefully pick your pupils who can cope with sitting at an angle to the board.
	POSTURES, POSITIONS & MOTOR SKILLS
B1	**Sitting posture** Despite correct seating and table height, the child still slumps over the desk, sprawls to the side or props their head or chin on hand, constantly fidgeting. This may indicate the need to improve the child's CORE STABILITY. If a child has poor posture and low muscle tone, writing takes more effort and is likely to cause fatigue. Improving core stability gives long term gains. See page 27 for more information on core stability. Try a 5 minute exercise programme (page 28) daily over 4-6 weeks to improve core stability which will in turn improve sitting posture.
B1 B2 B3	**Sloping boards** Scribes and calligraphers have used sloping boards for centuries. School children and architects have used sloped desks and for very good reason. It encourages the arm triangle for good movement, makes good upright posture easy and is maintainable over longer periods. Sloping boards can be used but perhaps as a last resort when other postural remedies have been tried. It is never best practice to have only one child in the class using a board, and it can be useful to have a few to share around the class so everyone can have a try. Sloping boards vary enormously. Sometimes just using a lever arch file under the pupil's work can help. Beware of manufactured boards with edges that can be uncomfortable to lean on. Our recommendation is for clear Perspex ones (available from Special Direct) which are less obvious and the child can place other work and their pencil case under it. Dycem non slip mats helps to stop work sliding around.
B2 B3 B9 C10	**Shoulder position** A raised shoulder position can be due to incorrectly sized furniture and incorrectly positioned paper/book. Shoulder stability is needed to enable the child to have one 'doing' hand and one 'helper' hand. Shoulder stability exercises should be done daily for 5 minutes over 2-4 weeks if you identify weakness in this area. See page 29 for targeted exercises.

Checklist	ENVIRONMENTAL
B4 B5 C10	**Wrist, Hand and Finger movements** In-hand manipulation skill has significant association with the handwriting skill level. (Cornhill & Case-Smith 1996) To develop fine finger movements, fluidity and accuracy of movements, practice activities which require a high degree of dexterity. **Activities** Bandage walk - pull in a long length of bandage, using the thumb to pull whilst anchoring fingers. Swap over to pulling the bandage in with fingers only whilst anchoring the thumb. Playdough - get beads/coins/counters out of the dough Coin line - turn over a line of coins as far as you can Threading - reels, large beads, small beads Twirl a pencil in one hand Move a coin from palm to fingertips Unwind nuts/bolts
B6	**Pencil Grip** The best way to teach correct grip is to do it properly from the start. Teach: PINCH YOUR PENCIL (between thumb and index) SIT IT DOWN ON YOUR MIDDLE FINGER READY TO WRITE! Each of the fingers on the pencil have a particular role to play: Thumb - initiates all circular movement Middle - stabilizes and supports the tripod grip Index - controls the movements All three are needed to contribute to fluid movement, and correct placement opens up the web space in the hand which also promotes good movement. Ways to help a child learn a tripod grip; - Blu tac on the pencil to place fingers on - Elastic band to guide position as a prompt - Triangular pencils - Wrist band bracelet to position pencil (make your own by linking rubber bands together). - Give a tissue pad to hold in 4/5th to hold against palm of hand. This helps develop a web space. - Place a clothes peg on a pencil so that once the pencil is gripped, the peg goes into the palm, again, encouraging a web space. Some children find this very comfortable. - Practice using tiny chalk pieces to encourage pincer grip writing Correct grip provides a web space which is vital in allowing circular hand movements. People use a wide variety of grip styles and it does not necessarily cause a problem. BUT where problems underlie in other areas of writing, a poor grip proves to be more important. Be aware that work will be slower and the child will give less consideration to spelling and sentence construction whilst they are concentrating on grip and formation.

Checklist	ENVIRONMENTAL
B6	**Changing grip** Incorrect grips are very hard to alter as the child adapts to the grip as a habit. However, speed and fluidity will always be compromised without a tripod grip. It is worth working on a better grip through KS1, but after this, unless a child is highly motivated, it is unlikely to be changed. Left handers often adopt a hooked grip. This is done as the child tries to see what they have written. If the paper is positioned properly, the left hander will be able to see their work without hooking their hand. However, many left handers report it is quite comfortable, no doubt, more comfortable than it looks! Starting out right forms good habits. Recommendation: "Write from the Start" - by Ion Teoderescu and Lois Addy (published by LDA). This is a whole programme devoted to developing all the movement and spacing skills required for handwriting without including letter formation. It is a very good starting point and is recommended for all Foundation and KS1 pupils. Practice tracking - dot to dots, doodle drawing, directional colouring, using templates and stencils. All these activities allow more concentration on pencil grip and accuracy of movement without having the added complication of letter formation.
B7	**Tension of Grip** Increased tightness in grip compromises movement and fluidity and leads to hand ache and fatigue. Consider: - Poor finger strength → work on hand skills - Suitability of pencil → try chunkier alternatives - Have they got a tripod grip → Work on tripod grip - without a web space, tension is increased unnecessarily - Where do they hold the pen? → Holding higher up the shaft can reduce tension - Are they anxious about writing? → Consider self-esteem/confidence
B8	**Hand Dominance** Hand preference starts at around 2 yrs. Dominance is likely to be well developed at school entry and fully developed by 7yrs. However, it is common in pupils with immature motor skills to be less established as bilateral integration is not developed fully (see Sections 1 and 2 of Start Write for more information). Advice: - without dominance, pupil highly unlikely to be ready for handwriting - continue lots of play which includes bilateral skills - rolling dough, cutting with scissors, threading and lacing cards, pouring, clapping games, construction toys, sand and water play. - Brain Gym - double doodles - Winding mechanical toys - Kinaesthetic activities ("Speed Up" by Lois Addy) Dominance WILL emerge in most cases, but if not, there will be evidence of other difficulties such as learning difficulties, spatial and body awareness issues or coordination disorders.

Checklist	ENVIRONMENTAL
B9	**Use of supporting hand** It is important to teach the use of the supporting hand. Activities such as cutting, lacing cards, stencils, construction toys encourage the active use of the non dominant hand.
B11	**Associated movements** Tongue poking/grimace/feet position/jaw moving? This is a normal reaction. It indicates increased effort, concentration and that the skill is still under development and is not yet refined or automatic. It indicates the need for more practice at this level so that the skill is consolidated and becomes automatic. NB. This may become a habit rather than a problem, but no adult wants to continue doing it, so maybe it's better to gently point out to older pupils so that they are more aware.
	THE FINISHED RESULT: THE WRITING PRODUCT
C1 C2 C3 C4 C5	**Letter formation** "If movement is made the top priority, children will need only to refine and speed up their writing with joins as they progress....Letters that move correctly can be neatened at any stage by slowing down .... Neat letters with an incorrect formation will prevent joining and cause faster writing to be illegible". (Sassoon) Teaching correct letter formation and being vigilant about it is possibly the most important area when considering handwriting development. **Multi-sensory learning** This is done very well in Foundation level, but tends to get a bit lost in later stages. If a child continues to have difficulties or struggles at the cursive stage, move away from pen and paper, and think in terms of movement and improve sensory processing (see page 24 for more ideas). Encourage: LARGE MOVEMENTS, SENSATION IN WRITING & FLUIDITY OF MOVEMENT - Teach letter families - see Section 7 in Start Write - Ribbon sticks and air writing - Stand to write BIG on whiteboard or paper on the wall - Chalk on paving stones - Water pistols on walls or playground - Torch shining on the wall - Gunge trays (or salt, or shaving foam) - Sand paper letters - Vocalisations! Meaningful ones! - Schemes which encourages laying down memory of phonics and shape such as Letterland and Callirobics (music and movement to letter sounds) - Start and Stop dots on letters - Rol n Write letters (available from LDA) - Handwriting sheets with a subtle letter and number line on for reference - Review problem letters - WATCH the child write - don't only assess from a writing sample

Checklist	ENVIRONMENTAL
C5	**Reversals** Reversals are normal when seen in children under 7yrs. If it is a major problem and persists after the age of 7yrs, it may indicate a visually based dysfunction. These children may also reverse whole words, or work R ⟶ L without realizing their error. They may not be aware of directionality and there may also be body awareness issues. Advice: - Revisit letter formation - Shadow matching letter to shape - Rol n Write letters - visually track and feel - Add commonly reversed letters into handwriting patterns eg. adadad bpbpbp - Teach "tricks" - little 'b' is same as capital B without the top circle b = bat and ball d = drum and stick c comes before d - so write a c and add a stick - Worksheets - pick out the correctly formed letters from the reversed ones and pick out reversed letters within words - Look at their own work with them and ask them to circle or identify any reversals. They may need a letter reference sheet to check against - Provide a reference grid of letters or numbers that they reverse on their desk, ruler, or inside an exercise book cover
C6 C7	**Spacing** Spacing makes work more legible - and the child needs to understand the reason why we do it! - Use stickers and blocks for each word - Try a "golden finger" as a fun reminder - Write an imaginary 'o' between words - Multi-sensory work is still of benefit - try making a sentence of plastic letters and remembering spaces - Correct a worksheet which has no spacing between words. Make one up using information about the topic that the class is doing (see Worksheets pages 93 - 94 for examples). - Make it relevant - Using a computer can reinforce the need for spacing and using the space bar gives a sensory reminder
C8	**Mixing Upper and Lower Case Letters** - This is often because a child is unsure of letter formation - so check their knowledge of the letters that they use in capital form or vice versa - Check their understanding of the correct use of capital letters - Make a worksheet related to a school topic where the child has to identify where capitals should be and spot where they are incorrectly used (see Worksheets pages 90 - 92)

Checklist ENVIRONMENTAL

C9 Punctuation

Develop funny actions for punctuation. Make it fun to add them to your work. Encourage using these movements in interaction with pupils when planning sentences. This maintains the input of sensory information and will help to remind the children to use it.

C10 Consistency

Fatigue, poor posture and unhelpful tools all need to be considered if a child's writing is extremely variable.

C11 Pencil Pressure

Heavy pressure can be the result of poor Proprioception (knowledge of position of body and strength of movement) or poor muscle tone, so the child grips very tightly and therefore applies too much pressure.
Anxiety causes tension and over pressure.
Light pressure can be the result of poor shoulder stability, low muscle tone and weak grip.
Consider:

- Improving/adjusting the pencil grip
- Working on shoulder stability (see page 27)
- Working on hand skills (see page 30)
- Fun tasks - such as colouring, tracing, scratch board pictures, writing through layers of carbon paper to either increase or decrease the mark that is made on the paper
- Use hand activities - to relax the hand and to balance out the use of the muscles in the hand
- Stretch the hand out to reduce tension - place hands under thigh to stretch forearm
- Shake out tension

C12 C1 Cursive

Cursive writing should not be taught until all letters are being formed correctly.
When teaching cursive right from the beginning, letters are less likely to be formed incorrectly and this can be an advantage of this scheme.
A review of the individual child will be helpful to focus on any letters which need attention before introducing cursive.

Printing		Cursive
Child learns a single letter form which improves simple recognition. Printing resembles what the child sees in reading books. It is the required writing for completing forms. Lifting off the page can interrupt thought processes and general fluency	VS	The child learns to deal with words as units and looks at the whole word which may help with spelling and spacing. Less easy to reverse letters. If you only learn cursive, you only learn to write ONCE. Faster and more fluid.

Checklist	ENVIRONMENTAL
C12 C1 (cont'd)	When a pupil is having difficulty learning cursive;- Check letter formation (WATCH THEM!) ▪ Practice letter joins found in their name: Ja Ja am me es Jam ame mes James James ▪ Practice cursive joins of high frequency words e.g. he, she, and, the, in, on, is ▪ Copy work from print rather than add the issue of planning, sequencing and forming sentences. ▪ Mark work for correct joins as well as spelling ▪ Same principle as learning print: KEEP LARGE and use MULTI SENSORY ▪ Re-assess their tools - is a change of pen required? ▪ Remember self-esteem issues as some children will still be using a pencil when everyone else is using a pen.
C13 C1	**Size of Writing** ▪ Return to practising size consistency in pencil patterns. ▪ Draw a highlighter line in which to write. Reduce depth of line for smaller letters. ▪ Child is likely to write their name in the size that is their natural preference. Take note of this, and check that it compares with the size that you are requesting. Try to use the size of lined paper that works for them and attempt as far as possible to be child centred in these choices. ▪ Use progressively smaller stickers. One word per sticker.
C14	**Endurance** ▪ Consider shoulder stability, pencil grip ▪ Pressure of grip on pencil ▪ General level of concentration ▪ Accurate and automatic knowledge of letter formation? ▪ Can the child rely on kinaesthetic and proprioceptive senses? Do they have to look at their hand whilst writing?
C15 C14	**Speed** Slower speed of writing may match the speed that the child is processing and planning information. Automaticity is required. Speed is not going to happen while the child still has to think and recall how to form a letter. Spelling knowledge is also going to effect speed. Some older children develop odd styles of forming some letters in attempts to be individual or to make their writing more attractive. This can become quite elaborate and may need discussion if speed is an issue. They may like to keep their individual styles for their best writing and return to simpler letter formations for speed writing and note taking.

GENERAL ADVICE

Copying

Potential difficulties include:

- Rapid looking up and down, copying two letters at a time.
- Struggling to relocate where they were copying from.
- Making errors - skipping words or even whole lines out.
- Not keeping up with peers.

Advice:

- Children who have difficulty copying MUST sit straight with the board and not at an angle.
- Reduce the amount of head movement by sitting them in the middle of the room rather than at front, and by being straight in front of the board.
- A sloping board can also help to reduce head movement.
- Provide points of reference; coloured lines, underline key words, provide large spacing.
- Suggest slower copiers, just copy underlined key words.
- It may be easier to copy from a worksheet.
- Major difficulties require a worksheet with just blanks to fill in.
- Write homework on the board at the start of the lesson to allow opportunity time to copy.
- Regularly photocopy a peer's neat copy for any child who requires it and leave a pile on the desk.

Left Handers

Left handers pull rather than push letters and it is a different movement. They also write towards the midline opposed to away from it.

Try to model position, pencil grip and movement by using your left hand (even if your writing with your left is poor!).

Left handers tend to hold the pencil slightly more upright in order to see what they are writing. They benefit from harder pencils (H or 2H) to avoid smudging, or quick drying ink pens. Also consider encouraging the pen or pencil to be held slightly higher up the shaft so that the child can see what they are writing. Remember the need to position the paper correctly, which also helps with seeing their work as it's written. Hook grips result from poor paper placement, and the need to see what they are writing.

Consider where you sit a left handed child. Sit left handers next to each other, or to the left of a right hander to avoid elbow wars!

Equipment:

Left handed scissors are basic equipment for every classroom.

Left handers tend to draw a line from Right to Left, giving more control as they pull towards themselves. Rulers for left handers are available numbered from right to left for easier measuring.

When copying work or patterns or letter formation, provide an example for the left hander on the RIGHT side of the paper so they can see what they are doing.

General Advice

Provide a good example and ensure all writing in exercise books, on the whiteboard and on displays all follow your writing scheme.

TEACH the need for good writing, the benefits of writing letters properly and using a good pen or pencil. It is an important life skill.

TEACH the need for two types of writing: one for best and one for speed.

Consider giving a mark for work and a mark for effort of writing.

Show particular interest in those children who are having difficulty with writing, so that you can notice and praise improvement.

Consider self esteem issues and how criticism of writing can be felt so personally at whatever age.

Be vigilant about other difficulties you observe such as unusual posture or tilting of the head and needing to be close to the board

Be aware of a new child who has learned an alternative writing scheme and may need additional input. If it is functional, does it really need changing?

2. HOW TO REVIEW AND ASSESS HANDWRITING PROGRESS

Improving across the whole school

This may be an area that you wish to address as a class teacher, SENCo, or Headteacher. At a point where your school is re-evaluating the approach to literacy it can be extremely enlightening to assess and audit how the entire school is performing. One way to do this could be by a whole class or whole school audit.

Why not consider auditing annually:

- How many children hold their pencil correctly?
- How many children are sitting correctly for a writing task? (Feet on floor, knees at 90°, back supported with table at correct height).
- Speed of handwriting over a 10 minute copying task?
- Correct use of punctuation over a carefully constructed paragraph?

You might also like to consider a more subjective audit:

- How many children like handwriting (and why)?
- How many parents agree that they had sufficient input and information about letter formation with regard to helping with homework?
- Do pupils like using the writing and colouring equipment that is provided in their classroom?

Audit information can provide a clear pathway to develop improvements across the whole school. It can highlight the importance of writing skill, and support your work in encouraging children to take pride in how they present their work.

Audit also provides an objective measure to reassess at a later date. Can you measure your improvements? Are pupils enjoying writing more? Has the quality of writing improved?

Improving with an individual child

Once you have started working on a child's handwriting, you are going to need to review your programme of intervention, and to assess the child's specific progress. Is your intervention making any difference?

It's good practice at this stage to reflect on what you are doing and make sure that you are going in the right direction.

Checklist:

- Decide on a time scale. When will intervention be evaluated?
- Refer back to your original assessment. What are you doing this for? Be specific!
- Ensure your handwriting targets tie in very closely with relevant IEP targets.

Informal assessment

Use a "first of the month" sheet, where the child copy writes the same sentence on the first possible day of each month on the same sheet of paper. This gives a month by month record of progress. It also provides a wonderful sample to laminate and present to the child at the end, so they can clearly see the changes that they have made.

At the end of handwriting intervention, show the child a piece of work they completed last term. Let them mark it for spacing, capitals or whatever their specific target has been. They may then make their own new targets to work towards, or choose out of a selection of targets which is the most important one that they wish to improve.

More formal assessment

If you have worked on a six week handwriting programme (see page 63), has the child achieved the set targets?

Quantity assessment

This simply means analysing a piece of work. For example, if they are working on spacing, how many correct spaces have they made in 100 words? Compare this at the beginning of intervention and at the end.

If the child is working on placing correct capitals, calculate how many capitals there should be in a correct piece of work, and count how many the child has achieved.

Speed of writing

There are a range of more complex timings for age, including words per minute and letters per minute. We have simplified it here to the grid below. Do bear in mind that particularly, younger children will vary speed considerably between copy writing and free writing. This affects the numbers so, always take this as a broad recommendation for speeds and compare different types and lengths of work.

Age	6yrs	7yrs	8yrs	9yrs	10yrs	13yrs	16yrs
Words per minute	4	6	7	9	10	15	20

Further detailed information about required writing speed with regard to access arrangements can be found at http://www.qca.org.uk

At Key Stage 1, children cannot have scribes or helpers for writing tasks.

At Key Stage 2, any pupil with a Statement of Special Educational Need can be given 25% extra time for written tasks. In any other case, where a school feels that the pupil requires more time, they have to request specific permission. This may be indicated where there is a free writing speed of 10 words per minute or fewer.

At Key Stage 3, a pupil is expected to have a free writing speed of at least 15 words per minute. If fewer than this, they may be eligible for extra time in access arrangements, but this does have to have been documented as an issue throughout the school year, and not just thrown in 2 weeks before applying!

Testing speed of writing

Compare speed of writing in a variety of settings:

- Copy writing (short)
- Copy writing (long duration i.e. over 10 minutes)
- Free writing (short)
- Free writing (long duration - of at least 15 minutes for KS2 and older children)
- Work done in a quiet environment compared to in a busy classroom

In longer pieces of work, you may wish to compare the quality of handwriting at the beginning, to the quality of the handwriting at the end.

Assessment - How quickly do you write?

This is an assessment to use once basic handwriting skills are established. It provides a measurable sample of writing which can be assessed for quality as well as speed. The use of a sentence containing every letter of the alphabet ensures that the assessor can check all letter formations, and in the case of an older child, can offer a good range of cursive joins.

Instructions:

The child can be given verbal instructions.

At the top, the child copies the sentence in their best writing, with no time limit.

In the lower box, the child then copies the sentence as many times as they can in 3 minutes. They should stop directly as instructed when 3 minutes is over.

HOW QUICKLY DO YOU WRITE?

Name: ____

Date: ____

FIRST OF ALL, DO YOUR BEST WRITING (NOT TIMED):

The five boxing wizards jump quickly.

NOW WRITE AS MANY AS YOU CAN IN 3 MINUTES!

The five boxing wizards jump quickly.

Note: Please use words per minute as a guideline

Total number of words per minute=

Comments:

Age	6	7	8	9	10	13	16
Words per minute	4	6	7	9	10	15	20

Compare handwriting speed with typing speed

This may be applicable where a child is able to produce much better results when using a computer. In many instances at KS1 and KS2, a child is unlikely to be faster typing than they are writing. However, there are children who are really very good at typing, and have found that keyboard skills have enabled them to produce their best quality of work. If there are concerns about their handwriting speed, compare the time it takes to hand write versus the time it takes to type. Mark both pieces of work for quality. Can the child use capitals, punctuation and spacing accurately on the keyboard?

If the speed is better on the keyboard, this must be a good argument for allowing the child to produce as much of their work as is practicable on the computer. Homework, best work, work to be presented on the wall, are all good examples of ways to encourage the use of keyboard skills.

Assessment - How is my handwriting?

A child who is involved and interested in the whole process of improving their handwriting skills is much more likely to succeed. A child centred approach to target planning and choice is encouraged. This assessment provides the child an opportunity to self evaluate their skills associated with handwriting including how they use a ruler and if they sit well on the chair.

This quick checklist provides the child with an opportunity to select and prioritise any issues that they feel should be addressed. Power to the child!

HOW IS MY HANDWRITING?

Name: ________________________________

Date: ________________________________

		Yes	No
1.	I sit well at my table, with my feet on the floor.	☐	☐
2.	I place my paper at an angle.	☐	☐
3.	I remember to hold my pencil correctly.	☐	☐
4.	I hold my paper still with my other hand.	☐	☐
5.	I remember to sit all my letters on the line.	☐	☐
6.	I keep my letters all the same size.	☐	☐
7.	I form all my letters correctly.	☐	☐
8.	I make all my tall letters tall enough.	☐	☐
9.	I make all the letters with tails go under the line.	☐	☐
10.	I remember to make spaces between every word.	☐	☐
11.	I use capital letters where I should.	☐	☐
12.	I always remember to put a full stop when I need to.	☐	☐
13.	I keep my writing horizontal on plain paper.	☐	☐
14.	I write right up to the margin.	☐	☐
15.	I use a ruler carefully.	☐	☐
16.	I can write without smudging.	☐	☐
17.	I can always read my own writing.	☐	☐
18.	My teacher can always read my writing.	☐	☐
19.	I think I write as fast as I need to in class.	☐	☐
20.	I like my writing. I think its neat and nice to look at.	☐	☐

3. DEVELOPING A SIX WEEK PROGRAMME

Having a pre-planned programme in your filing cabinet, ready to bring out for use is an invaluable addition to your resources.

Why six weeks? A short block helps focus on targets. Programmes that go on for too long lose appeal and interest. Children benefit from knowing when it is going to end, otherwise it may feel a never ending uphill journey.

Sessions should be for a group of no more than six children, and four is more manageable for one person, particularly if your format is for a teaching assistant to work with a small group outside the classroom.

Plan for each session to last no more than 40 minutes. This should include movement, the development of physical skills such as shoulder stability, or hand dexterity. It should also include quick changing brief activities so that pupils maintain interest and concentration.

Be clear and specific with your instructions. Try not to fall into the trap of repeating instructions using different language in an attempt to help the pupils understand. Don't give the children two mystifying sets of instructions for the same task! It is more effective to keep the instructions short, and repeat the instruction using the same language.

It would be easy for us to provide you with a completed six week programme, but we are talking about a specific programme, based around policy principles of your school. The range of handwriting schemes and policies are wider than ever, so providing a programme that meets your particular needs is very difficult.

Advice:

- The most useful way to work on programme development is to have clear targets. Keeping these targets small and achievable is the most effective way to motivate pupils and to build confidence.
- Consider your range of tools and equipment. Plan ahead for appropriate equipment which will be motivating and provide a fresh direction for pupils. Plain

paper and wooden crayons are pretty boring! Writing with ribbons, writing to music, squirting letter formation with water pistols and using gunge is much more memorable! Financial outlay can reap dividends in the long term to promote interest and enjoyment makes attending a handwriting group much more fun for your pupils!

- Introduce new methods that the pupils have not come across before. Self-evaluation, marking their own work, choosing how to receive rewards for good work, and developing their own targets can all be ways of underlining the importance of the life skill of handwriting.
- Gather all your equipment together in a box for each week. Have preparation time at the beginning of the programme so that everything is ready. Don't leave it to rushing around at the last minute each week, trying to find tools, and then ending up making do with something else. This is important. It needs to be organized, well presented and well evaluated in order for it to have its full benefit for the pupils.
- Swap or borrow resources from other schools. This may just mean borrowing books, or to have a trial run with a resource before you buy one for your own school. Share your experiences with fellow teachers. Consider setting up a Handwriting Interest Group in your local cluster of schools. A colleague may have already prepared the resources that you are looking for. Share! Perhaps you could discuss having a small joint budget to share among a cluster of schools.
- And...... if you have a great idea, and you are unable to source it anywhere to purchase, contact companies like Special Direct (www.specialdirect.com) who may be able to manufacture this, and in turn, raise funds for your school.
- Be creative with your motivators! Discuss with your group of pupils what rewards they would like. Extra time on the computer on Friday afternoon can be good. Perhaps being able to help with an art/craft session with a younger class might be a really good "carrot". Make rewards meaningful for your pupils. Stickers are valued by younger children but, by the time they have acquired several books of them, they cease to have much appeal. On the other hand, working towards a goal that is pleasurable and exciting is likely to be much more motivating.

The following pages show an example of the detail we suggest you work through and plan for your sessions plus a template to create your own.

Week One

Aims: To develop fluency of pencil movement

Target(s): That pupils can accurately copy three writing patterns of one line length

Equipment: Assorted pens, chunky markers, sand tray, ribbon sticks, whiteboard and A3 paper

Warm-ups: warm up sheet, Brain Gym, cross march and hook ups for listening

Teaching methods: demonstration, movement to music, hand over hand guidance, sky writing, encourage choice of pens, vocalisations to match movements

Activities: check pencil grip

Skywriting copying patterns on board

Copy partner - mirror movement - guess which pattern

Turntaking with sand tray

whiteboard patterns

write from the start pages.....

Complete pre-writing sheet A

Feedback and Praise: each pupil chooses and rings best work and shows group. Photocopy to take home.

Evaluation: (continue overleaf)

SIX WEEK HANDWRITING PROGRAMME

Week: Date:

Aims:

Target(s):

Equipment:

Warm-ups:

Teaching methods:

Activities:

Feedback and Praise:

Evaluation: (continue overleaf)

4. INTRODUCING IT

It is a common worry that introducing computers and keyboards will take away the child's opportunity to develop their handwriting skills. This is almost always unfounded. Pencil and paper is always going to be the preferred method for a quick note, form filling and when a computer is not available.

Even when a decision has been made to increase a child's access to IT, handwriting continues to be required and the child should continue with their skill development with pencil skills in all areas.

However, the use of a computer can often provide a positive alternative for the pupil who has been consistently struggling to record their knowledge through handwritten work. Children easily become disheartened and lose confidence when they see their peers producing handwriting which is more legible and easy to read than their own.

In this age of technology, it seems a small step to make allowances for certain pupils to have increased access to computers. Parents can help by supporting their child in learning keyboard skills and early typing skills through fun, early learning software.

It is important to be aware that typing out work is rarely quicker during the Primary School stage. It is not going to provide an overnight solution. However, it is important to introduce this early on if it is a realistic requirement for the child. Another pre-requisite is having a good, functional level of hand skills and dexterity. The child who has great difficulty isolating finger movement is unlikely to cope well with typing.

A good recommendation is that if IT is going to be required, it should be introduced and supported in school by Years 4 and 5. The child should be encouraged to develop good keyboard skills and habits right from the beginning. Basic word processing such as how to save and print without adult input is a very important skill.

Advice for introducing IT

- Check that furniture is appropriately sized, providing good support and a good postural position. The child also needs to have good visual access. Make sure that the screen and keyboard are in a good position. The keyboard should be placed so that the arms are well supported, and the hands are in a functional position ready for typing. The screen should not be too far away, but should also not be dictating the position of the keyboard.

- High stools, office chairs and benches don't often provide sufficient postural support. The same principles are required in supportive seating at the computer, as are required for correct posture at a normal desk.
- Engage parents in encouraging their child, and where possible to provide access to a computer with relevant software. Schools are sometimes able to provide samples of the software that is used in the classroom.
- Test the speed of handwriting versus the speed of typing by timing same copied sentences. Repeat this at regular intervals to review how the use of IT is affecting performance. It may be that it is not required and is merely adding another task onto a crammed curriculum for this pupil.
- De-activate unnecessary keys. You can also consider covering unused keys.

- Modify the "press and hold" function in order to stop repeated letters being entered accidentally.
- Enlarge the font if appropriate. Choose an appropriate font such as comic sans.
- Always print out work to check. It is easier to check on a hard copy.
- Use simple predictive software to increase speed. Freeware can easily be found on the internet. Have clear rules about when spellchecker can be used. It is appropriate not to use it in Literacy lessons so that the child works on their spelling alongside peers.
- Practice (and teach) how to use a spell checker properly.
- Consider using different peripheral equipment such as a tracker ball mouse or a key guard.
- If copying work, use a vertical document holder.
- Allow homework to be typed as a matter of course.
- Ensure that the pupil can save, retrieve and print work independently.
- Explain to peers that this pupil has targets connected with using IT and it something that they need to do, rather than just favouritism.
- Consider how to integrate the consistent use of IT into school life for this child. Consider access to printers, paper, and how to problem solve.
- Plan a six week or similar length programme to structure the pupils IT skills. This may be a programme that is kept and used for any pupils who have IT requirements.
- Discuss with the Headteacher how problems with the computer will be resolved. Some schools employ an IT support assistant. It is not always possible for a class teacher to take on this role.

5. A GREAT EXAMPLE OF WORKING WITH OLDER PUPILS

On one of our training days for Handwriting, we met a teacher called Sam Brown. Sam is a Year 6 Teacher at Serlby Park (3-18 Business and Enterprise Learning Community) in Nottinghamshire. Sam attended the course as she was the member of staff nominated and responsible for handwriting programmes within the school. She attended the course with her colleague, Paul Farman, a Year 6 teacher at the same school.

Their perspective on developing good handwriting skills right from the beginning was really interesting and unusual. Their school potentially has a child right from nursery through to A Levels, and is one of the first schools in the country to work in this way. As a result, they have a huge 'buy in' for getting it right in the first place, as without good basic skills, their school is having to spend extra time and resources later on to remediate these difficulties. Its not like an Infant School that can pass its problems onto Juniors and so on!

They were an inspirationally enthusiastic pair of teachers and explained their intention to return to school after the training and completely re-evaluate how pupils are introduced to handwriting.

They shared with us information about a super project that they had started recently, which was encouraging Year 6 pupils to improve their handwriting. It took the form of a 'Handwriting League' which aimed to focus pupil's attention on the standard of their handwriting, whilst making it fun, and clearly offering strategies and ways to improve. The Handwriting League raised the profile of handwriting, whilst at the same time encouraging the pupil's own responsibility to engage and improve. Confidence and self esteem levels increased and, alongside this, the handwriting noticeably improved too. What an achievement!

Here's what Sam said about it:

Handwriting Football League

Samantha Brown - TLR 1 Core Skills, Year 6 teacher. Serlby Park (3-18 Business and Enterprise Learning Community)

Serlby Park opened in September 2005 as a Business and Enterprise Learning Community for learners aged 3 to 18. It was an amalgamation of the three local schools. Most learners come from Bircotes and Harworth, a socially disadvantaged area on the outskirts of Nottinghamshire. The proportion with learning difficulties or disabilities is above average along with those entitled to free school meals. This is a familiar story amongst schools in traditional mining communities along with the other common complaint - low self-esteem.

For more details and great photos of the children's handwriting league, please see www.thelocaltherapycompany.co.uk

We found that many of the children in Year 6 did not value their own work. They believed themselves to be 'rubbish' or 'thick' when really their work was well written to a satisfactory and even high standard.

When we asked the children why they thought that they were 'rubbish' a common theme emerged. 'It looks rubbish' , 'It's scruffy' , 'It's a mess' The children judged themselves to be 'rubbish' at writing because of the way it looked - not by what they had written. This was especially evident amongst the boys.

Children throughout their entire school life are often judged on appearances. How smart they look, how the school looks and how their work looks. Many of the children write really good, high level pieces of work but they are judged on the appearance of the work. If it is hard to read, then people don't want to read it. I'm guilty of this myself, always putting the 'scruffy' books to the bottom of the pile, leaving them until last, then, when I get to them I always feel disheartened because I know that there will be some bits of their work that I will just skim over rather than try and decipher what it says. Do external English examiners at all levels KS2, KS3 KS4 and beyond have the same 'sinking feeling' when it comes to 'scruffy' work. Does this affect the written mark?

The teachers of Year 6 decided that something needed to be done to help improve handwriting and children's self esteem before it was too late -and so the Handwriting Football League was born.

A large display board in a prominent position along the corridor turned into a football pitch complete with accurately marked out lines. It had an immediate effect. Even before the children knew what it was for there was a buzz around Year 6. Children were stopping in front of the board in groups and speculating why there was a large football pitch on the wall, then over the next few days as the labels, example handwriting and finally the title was attached to the board the interest grew and grew.

In the meantime we had asked each child in Year 6 to write out the same piece of handwriting and mount it on coloured card themselves, but we still hadn't told them what the football pitch was for or why they had written out a piece of text that had no link to any topics we were covering. We had them intrigued!

We now needed to hook into their intrigued thoughts and capture their interest. We gave each child a football with their name on, took them out into the corridor and explained exactly how the football handwriting league worked. Being in Year 6 we used examples of handwriting from past SATs papers along with the descriptions from the mark schemes. We did not alter the descriptions to 'child speak' because we wanted the children to be aware of exactly what a SATs marker was looking for.

We then explained that the examples were categorized into leagues - Premiership, Championship, Division 1, Division 2. Each child then took their own handwritten piece and matched it to the descriptions and examples of handwriting and placed their football on the appropriate league. This was designed to be a self assessment program for their own handwriting but what also happened is that children were peer assessing and discussing in groups each other's handwriting and coming to group decisions about assessment. The children then went on and encouraged each other to improve and gave advice to children in the lower leagues.

Top Tip: Why not run a training academy for Division 2 handwriters to work on their skills to gain promotion

In the following weeks, the initial excitement died down. The children had three very short formal lessons on handwriting to remind them about how letters join but that was it. The teachers decided not to teach handwriting and just experiment with self esteem. Does the fact that the children now know what is expected of them raise their level of handwriting? Does the little reminder and praise from the teacher about handwriting enthuse them? Are they now being encouraged by their peers?

The answer to all these questions revealed themselves three months later when we asked the children to write out the same piece of handwriting again. With virtually no teaching of handwriting, most children had improved. The most significant changes and improvements were made by the boys.

What was also very interesting was that when the children initially placed their footballs on the league table some of them had misplaced themselves. The ones with really low self esteem had automatically placed themselves in division 2 without really looking at the description or comparing their own handwriting, whilst the ones with over inflated egos had placed themselves in the premiership! Both groups of children had to go back and re-assess their work with help from their peers and teachers. Three months on the same children had really looked carefully at the descriptions and placed themselves in the correct league the first time.

Across the whole year group, the children's perception of their own handwriting is now more accurate and the general standard of writing has risen. The most important thing to come out of this project is that the children now think that they are better at writing then they were three months ago, their self esteems have risen and they spend more time thinking about what they write instead of worrying about the way that they write it.

They are much happier writers. Raising the profile of handwriting really works to improve standards.

6. WHEN TO REFER TO OUTSIDE AGENCIES

- Major perceptual issues - if a child has enjoyed a broad spectrum of play activities and benefited from multi-sensory learning, then perceptual development should be on track. If a child has extreme or consistent difficulty in acquiring letter formation or persists with reversals, or writing from right to left, then further advice needs to be sought.
- Motor difficulties - such as very poor hand function, poor gross motor skills or indeed a physical disability will all affect handwriting and further advice may be beneficial.
- Despite increased efforts and individualised teaching, if a child's ability is falling way behind their peer group, an Educational Psychology assessment may be required.
- If a child is having difficulty writing, but their performance in others areas such as maths and science is good, or their verbal ability exceeds their written ability, further assessment is needed.

WORKSHEETS

Match the letter to its shadow Pages 76 - 77

It can be helpful to have some resources at hand to help a child recognise different letters. Some children will learn letter shapes by outlines, and words by their outline shapes.

Included here, are some shapes, to copy, cut out, laminate and use for a matching activity. You will need to mark the bottom of each letter with a colour, so that p and b do not get mixed up and so on. You could, of course, make a whole alphabet of letters and shadows - be sure to reflect the writing style that you are teaching.

Spacing, copy and accuracy worksheets Pages 78 - 95

Accuracy in looking and ability to process information visually is vital in successful handwriting. This group of samples provide ideas for developing these skills.

Please note the worksheets on pages 85 and 88 are specifically designed for use with left-handed writers.

MATCH THE LETTER TO ITS SHADOW

Cut out and then match the letters to the shadow

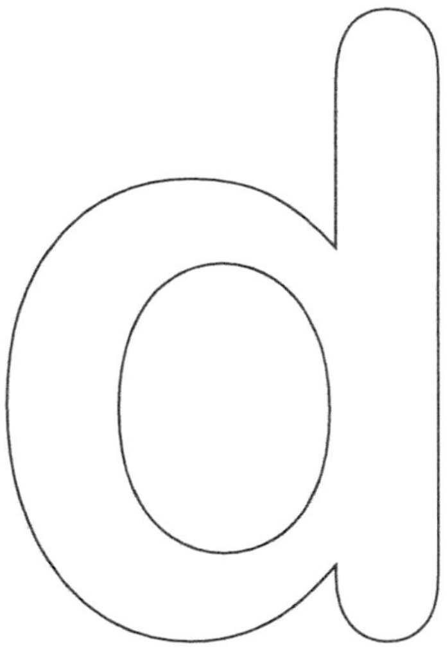

MATCH THE LETTER TO ITS SHADOW

Cut out and then match the letters to the shadow

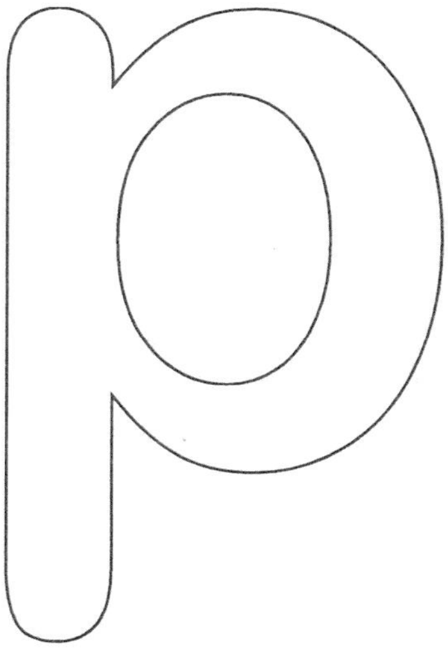

GRIDS!

Copy the patterns from grids on the left to the blank grids on the right. Remember to look carefully and draw accurately!

GRIDS!

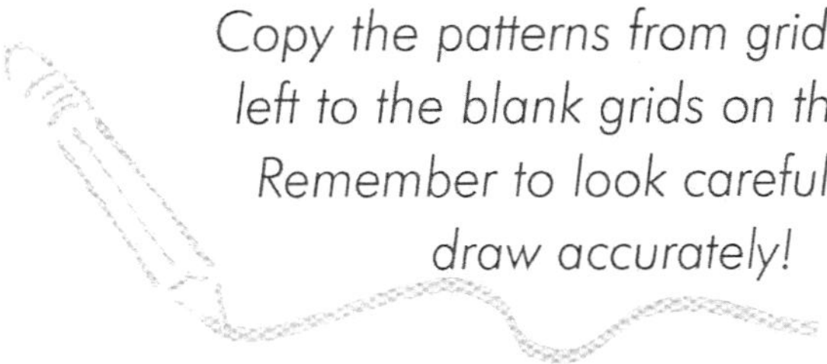

Copy the patterns from grids on the left to the blank grids on the right. Remember to look carefully and draw accurately!

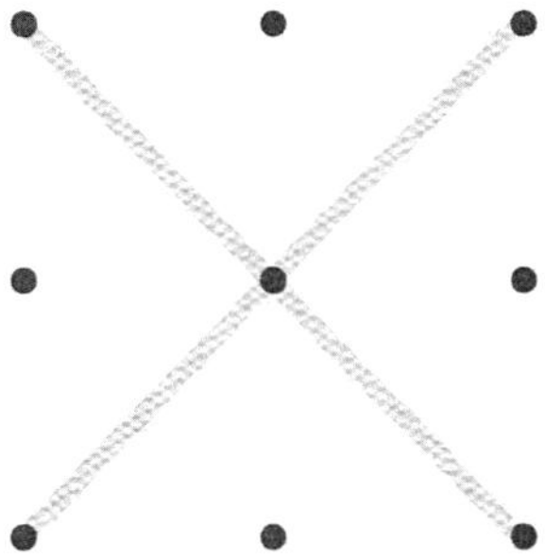 

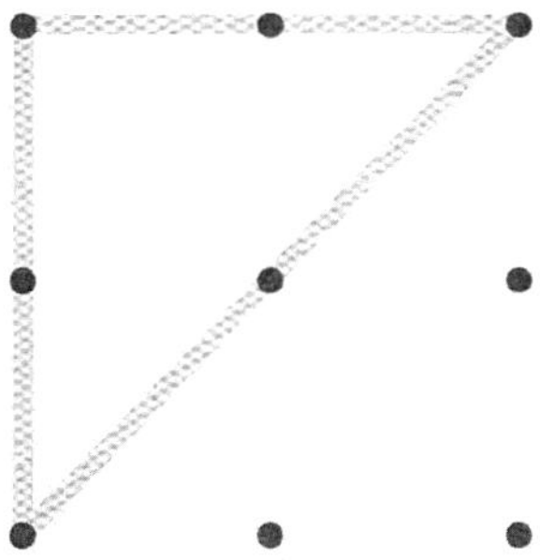 

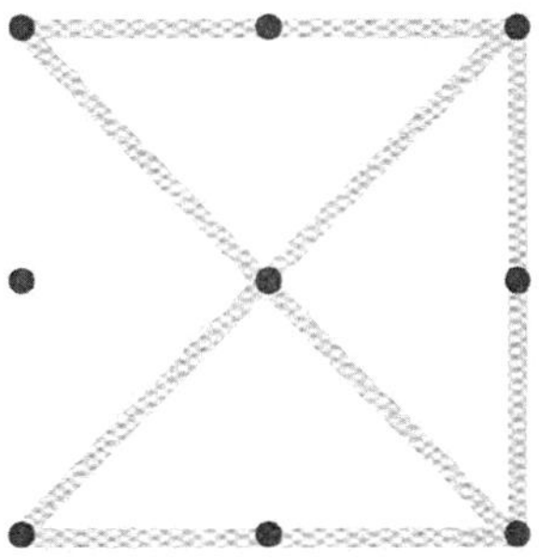 

GRIDS!

Make up some of your own patterns on the grids below!

TRICKY GRIDS!

Copy the patterns from grids on the left to the blank grids on the right. Remember to look carefully, draw accurately and use a ruler!

TRICKY GRIDS!

Copy the patterns from grids on the left to the blank grids on the right. Remember to look carefully, draw accurately and use a ruler!

TRICKY GRIDS!

Make up some of your own patterns on the grids below.

HALF PICTURES - RIGHT HANDED!

Carefully draw the missing half of the pictures below.

HALF PICTURES - LEFT HANDED!

Carefully draw the missing half of the pictures below.

COPY THE PICTURES

Carefully draw the pictures on the left into the blank box on the right hand side of the page.

PENCIL PATTERNS!

Continue the patterns carefully, keeping the same size and on the line. Take your time and make sure your fingers are doing all the work.

PENCIL PATTERNS!

Continue the patterns carefully, keeping the same size and on the line. Take your time and make sure your fingers are doing all the work.

For left-handed writers

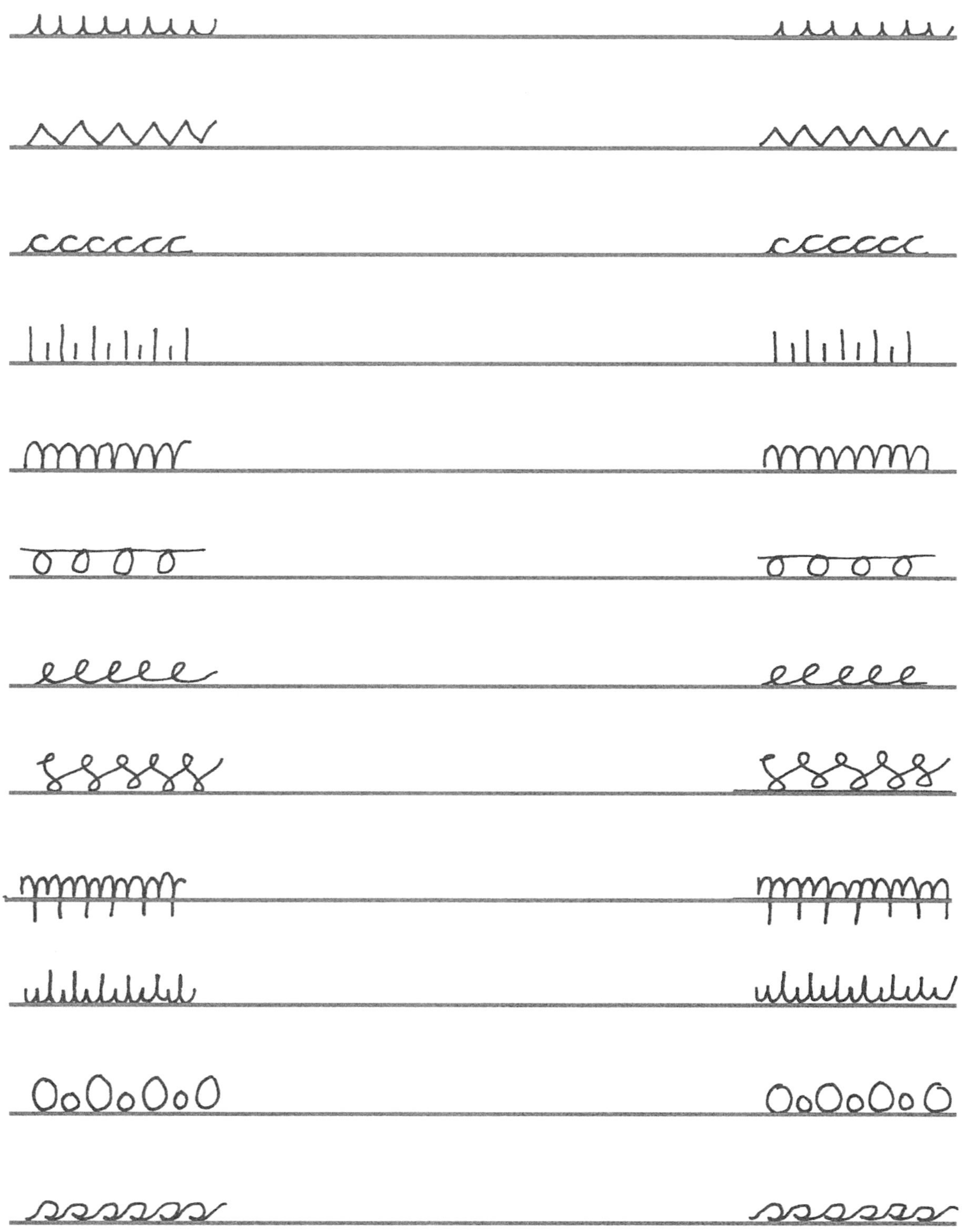

LETTER SOUNDS!

Can you match each letter to another letter which has the same sound? Watch out! These are mixtures of all sorts of ways to write the letters and even some capitals mixed in!

a i H j K b

A q m h f e

r g B f B y e

q m B t s i w

H W Y f g i

k r A b f B

y e q m B t s i

a i H j K b A

q m h f e A

WHEN TO USE CAPITAL LETTERS

- Names of people and places
- At the start of each new sentence
- Title and date

Circle the words that should have a capital letter.

late	april	america
sam	walking	toby
door	alice	struggled
england	beach	sea
school	peter	july
box	rodney	suitcase
seagull island	paper	strawberry
ferry	martha	dinner

WHEN TO USE CAPITAL LETTERS

- Names of people and places
- At the start of each new sentence
- Title and date

Put in all the capital letters.

charlotte's hotel by james smith

19 june 2007

it took some time to get everybody into the ferry boat. it was a bit of a squeeze. they were all just getting comfortable when gemma realised she had forgotten her hat. she had left it in her car. then two of the children said they felt sick before rodney had even started the engine. at last they were settled and the boat sailed across to seagull island. charlotte was waving to them from the shore.

WHEN TO USE CAPITAL LETTERS

Can you add the capital letters to these paragraphs?

Remember.....

- Place names.....such as Scotland
- Proper names...like Alice
- Beginning of a sentence
- Watch out for important words that might need capital letters too!

my first trip to london - by george jones

the first time i ever went to london, i went with my grandma peters and my little sister, grace. dad drove us down to the railway station and left the three of us to start our adventure.

we went down lots of steps to a special sort of train called the underground. this goes right underneath all the roads and gets you to where you want to go without having to get stuck in traffic jams. it was a very bumpy ride and grandma peters nearly fell into a lady's lap. grace and i laughed, but grandma looked a bit cross. later on we found out that she had also managed to squash our sandwiches. yuk!

the first place we went to was buckingham palace, that's where the queen lives by the way. her proper name is queen elizabeth the second. i wonder if her friends call her that? there are soldiers that stand outside the palace all day and all night, just to guard her and make sure she is safe. they aren't allowed to smile or talk to you. grace said she thought it was a boring job, but i liked their uniform.

the next place we went to was a special museum called madame tussaud's. it has lots of life size models of famous people made out of wax! i was standing in a room with david beckham, james bond and even ant and dec! it was amazing. grace hardly recognized any of the famous people, but then she is only little.

i had a brilliant time in london. hopefully, we will go again soon. grandma says there is lots more to see in england's capital city.

SPACE CHALLENGE!

Can you put a line between words where the spaces should be?

Ilikeplaytimesatschoolwhen MrsSmithcomestoorganise
games.Shebringsgreattoysandequipmentsothatthereis
alwayssomethingnewtotry.Iwantedtolearnhowtocatch
betterandnowIcan.Weplayedwithalovelyballthathad
streamersonitwhichmadeiteasytosee.NowIcancatcha
tennisballjustabouteverytime.Theothergamethatwe
learnedwithMrsSmithwasFrenchskipping.Youneeda
longpieceofelasticwhichistiedtogethertomakeabig
loop.Twopeoplestandinsidetheelastic,oneateachend
sothattheloopisspreadoutandisaboutonemetrelong.
Thenthepersonwhogetstohavethefunjumpsinandoutof
theloop.MrsSmithtaughtussomerhymestosaywhilewe
areplayingit.Havinggoodgamestoplayisgreatfun.Even
whenmybestfriendisbusyplayingwithsomeoneelse,Ican
goandjoininthegamesthatMrsSmithisorganising.Ithink
itsagreatideaandweallllikehercomingtohelpus.

Well done! That was hard wasn't it? That's how hard it is to read writing when the spaces aren't very clear.

WHERE ARE THE SPACES?

Put a bold, colourful line where the spaces should be.

Hello!MynameisOrlaIamaverybigdogIamblackandgreyand whiteandamusuallycoveredinmud.ThatsbecauseIlikerunning aroundinthefields.WhenIgethomeIamveryhungryandliketo haveabigdinnertoeat.

MyownersaysIamalazydog.Iliketosleepalldayonmyblanket,but mostofallIliketolieinfrontofthefire.InthesummerIsunbatheinthe gardenandwatchthechildrenplayinthepaddlingpool.Itlooksfun andIwouldliketojoinin,buttheydon'tseemtowantmeto!Theydo throwsticksandballsformetochasethoughandIreallylikethat!

Ifyoucanreadthisthenyouareverycleverbecausethespaceshavebeenleftoutandit makesitverydifficulttoread.Remembertoalwaysleaveaspacebetweenwords.

Remember to add spaces between every word you write!

ALPHABET SENTENCES

Copy the sentences in the spaces below. Take your time and write carefully! Let your fingers do all the work.

The five boxing wizards jump quickly.

We promptly judged antique ivory buckles for the next prize.

Five or six big planes zoomed quickly by the new tower.

Their kind aunt was subject to frequent dizzy spells, thus causing much anxiety and worry.

The new farmhand proved strong but lazy after having picked only six quinces.

USEFUL WEBSITES

Seat wedges www.backinaction.co.uk

Dot to dots, colouring resources www.edHelper.com

Make your own handwriting sheets

www.instructorweb.com/resources/handwriting.asp

Suppliers

Special Direct www.tts-group.co.uk/specialdirect - excellent range of handwriting resourc

Anything left-handed www.anythingleft-handed.co.uk

Taskmaster www.taskmasteronline.co.uk

Philip & Tacey Ltd www.philipandtacey.co.uk

If you have any feedback or anything you would like to share with us please get in touch!

www.tts-group.co.uk/specialdirect

www.thelocaltherapycompany.co.uk